Writing Off the
BEATEN TRACK

Contemporary Issues in the Middle East

Writing Off the BEATEN TRACK

Reflections on the Meaning of Travel and Culture in the Middle East

JUDITH CAESAR

Syracuse University Press

First Edition 2002
02 03 04 05 06 07   6 5 4 3 2 1

Mohamad El-Hindi Books on Arab Culture and Islamic Civilization are published with the assistance of a grant from Ahmad El-Hindi.

The paper used in this publication meets the minimum requirements of American National Standard for Information Sciences—Permanence of Paper for Printed Library Materials, ANSI Z39.48–1984.∞™

Library of Congress Cataloging-in-Publication Data
Caesar, Judith.
Writing off the beaten track : reflections on the meaning of travel and culture in the Middle East / Judith Caesar.—1st ed.
p. cm.—(Contemporary issues in the Middle East)
ISBN 0-8156-2957-5
1. United Arab Emirates—Social life and customs. 2. United Arab Emirates—Description and travel. 3. Caesar, Judith—Journeys—United Arab Emirates. I. Title. II. Series
DS247.T84 C34 2002
953.57—dc21   2002013529

Manufactured in the United States of America

Contents

PART FOUR Off the Beaten Track

Acknowledgments

I would like to thank the friends and colleagues who have read and commented on sections of the manuscript, particularly Alona Shepard, who took time from an incredibly hectic schedule to share her insights and suggestions with me. I also have greatly appreciated the encouragement and support of the acquisitions editor at Syracuse University Press, Mary Selden Evans. Finally, I would like to thank the American University of Sharjah for granting me the release time that enabled me to complete the manuscript on schedule. However, the opinions expressed in this work are, of course, my own personal responses and do not reflect the official policies or views of the university.

Judith Caesar was raised in Pennsylvania and has a doctorate in American literature from Case Western Reserve University. She has taught in Saudi Arabia, Egypt, China, Japan, and the United Arab Emirates. Her first book, *Crossing Borders: An American Woman in the Middle East,* was published by Syracuse University Press in 1997. Her essays have appeared in the *Progressive* and the *Christian Science Monitor,* and her short stories and creative nonfiction have been published in literary quarterlies such as the *Antioch Review,* the *Kansas Quarterly,* the *Massachusetts Review,* the *High Plain Literary Review,* the *Dalhousie Review,* and the *North American Review.* She is currently an associate professor of English at the American University of Sharjah in the United Arab Emirates.

Introduction

Why Don't You Just Stay Home?

I have spent a great deal of my life in places other Americans have never heard of. As a child, I lived for two years on a small Japanese island called Eta Jima, where my father was a dental officer at an American military base. I played with Japanese children, wore *geta* (thonged wooden sandals), spoke a little Japanese, and learned that there were religions called Buddhism and Shintoism. I heard the drums of the cherry blossom festivals and saw the fish-shaped kites flying over houses on Boy's Day. My mother had beautiful red flowered silk kimonos made for me, which I wore when we went into the village on festival days. I still have a picture of myself then, a little blue-eyed girl with a ponytail and a parasol, dressed in a kimono. Then I returned to the United States and found that none of my classmates had ever heard of Shintoism or Buddhism, nor were they impressed by my Japanese phrases. My new American friends sometimes talked about the "sneaky little Japs," which didn't sound to me much like my old Japanese playmates. The kimonos became Halloween costumes.

I adapted to being in the United States again easily

enough at the time. I didn't even realize that I had lost anything until much later when I was a college student taking creative writing courses. Even though I had spent most of my childhood in America, I wrote again and again about an American child living in Japan. When I tried to write about American teenagers growing up in America, as most of the other students did, I felt as if I were putting on an all-American mask and costume to try to crash their party. The experience of being both outside America and outside a foreign culture was more a part of me than I had thought.

Then the experience faded. In my twenties and thirties, I went to graduate school, taught at small Pennsylvania colleges, and watched the sixties and seventies pass, with all their political and social upheaval, feeling what many people of my generation felt. I wrote short stories about America that were competent, unstartling, and usually unpublished. My all-American costume had become my clothes.

The rest of my life could have continued in that vein if I hadn't been offered a teaching job in Saudi Arabia in 1980. I went to Saudi Arabia thinking what many Americans thought about Arabs and the Middle East. I left two years later with my stereotypes in the trash and my politics changed radically. I continued traveling and teaching in other countries—China, Japan, Egypt, and then back to Saudi Arabia again. I liked living in other cultures because it made me question what I thought I knew. I went on epistemological adventures. Before, my questions had come from the inconsistencies I could see from within my society; the basic values remained a given. But the moment one responds sympathetically to another culture is the moment one ceases to view her own society's habits and ideas as the only normal way to be. For me, travel was a literal experience of being alienated, first of being an alien in another culture, and then of living again in America after having had an experience that was alien to that of the other Americans with whom I lived and worked. Yet this alienation didn't bring the sense of loneliness and loss that the word usually connotes. I had to become an alien to see where I was.

When I finally returned to the United States, I didn't need to search for a subject to write about. I wrote about all that I had seen and done and felt in China and Japan and the Middle East because I wanted to share those experiences and insights with everyone who would listen. The short stories and essays I wrote were much better than those than I had written before because I had too much to say to keep to it all to myself.

But not everyone wanted to hear what I had to say. I realized this vividly a few years after I had come home, when I was being interviewed for a creative writing job at a small college in Wisconsin. The interviewer had asked me a question I hadn't expected, a question that, I think, embodies a certain American attitude toward foreign travel.

"You've seen so many exotic places," he began. "Wouldn't we seem awfully dull to you?"

I tried to explain that the mental journeys were important, not the physical ones, and that there were many ways that one could take mental journeys. A person could certainly be cultivated and sophisticated without traveling, I suggested, if he took the right kinds of mental journeys.

"Then why didn't you just stay home?" he wondered.

I think now, looking back, that the cards were stacked against me. If I said travel was enriching, I would be implying that my future colleagues were unenriched, and if I said that travel didn't matter, I sounded as if I had foolishly misspent my life. I think my travels had made me somewhat suspect in his eyes. I suppose he thought that I considered myself more sophisticated than he was because I had seen exotic places he had only read about. I wish I could have found a way of explaining that looking at the lovely scenery of a far-away country really means nothing. Scenery is scenery. Walking down the streets of a famous city is no more meaningful than shaking hands with a celebrity. The meanings are inside, as you redefine yourself against a background of different questions. But sometimes one has to take a physical journey in order to take a mental journey.

American academics are in a curious position concerning the rest of the world. We can pretend that the rest of the world doesn't exist if we want to. I don't think many intellectuals in other places can do the same. Certainly, third-world intellectuals can't ignore the rest of the world; the rest of the world controls their destinies. Most educated Europeans have at least some idea of what is going on in neighboring countries and speak a second language. But most of the American academics and writers that I know don't speak a second language and haven't lived in another culture.

Living in America, it isn't easy to find out about other societies. If we go into a library or bookstore, most of the books about other cultures are published in the United States, and almost all of the magazines and newspapers at the newsstands are American. Yet living in America and reading only what Americans have to say about the world is like going through life with a virtual reality headset clamped over your eyes and ears. We absorb images and meanings selected by other people, often people who want to sell us books and magazines and films by making us feel comfortable with what we already believe. We can come to think that America is the whole world and that what is outside the American experience is outside the human experience. All that we don't know can become suspect. This is one reason, I think, why one can't just stay home, or at least why I can't.

Americans have written beautiful books about staying at home and becoming one with a place: *Walden, Pilgrim at Tinker Creek, Dakota.* Yet these are great books because of the mental and spiritual places that the writers explored while staying home. Walden Pond and Tinker Creek and Dakota were stepping off points into the universe. Staying at home and traveling are not opposite impulses, but different routes to places of mind outside one's own time and place. Whether the mental journey has been long or short, and the thoughts lofty or earthly, it is the journey and what one brings back from it that matter.

The essays in this book are about the United Arab Emirates because this is where I live, and because this region has a history and a culture that has often been ignored or misrepresented. But more than being just descriptions and history or impressions of history, these essays are about the meaning of living in a place where an American will never quite belong, about what America looks like from the outside, and about the look and feel of the mental places where encountering differentness led me. These essays are a series of pictures on top of my picture of the Emirates. They bear the imprint of my mind trying to understand what it sees. Looking at these pictures together you may see not a virtual reality, but a three-dimensional image that will evoke a place of the mind.

PART ONE Places

Though the view from my door was still more contracted, I did not feel crowded or confined in the least. There was pasture enough for my imagination. . . . Both place and time were changed, and I dwelt nearer to those parts of the universe and to those eras of history that most attracted me.

—Thoreau, *Walden*

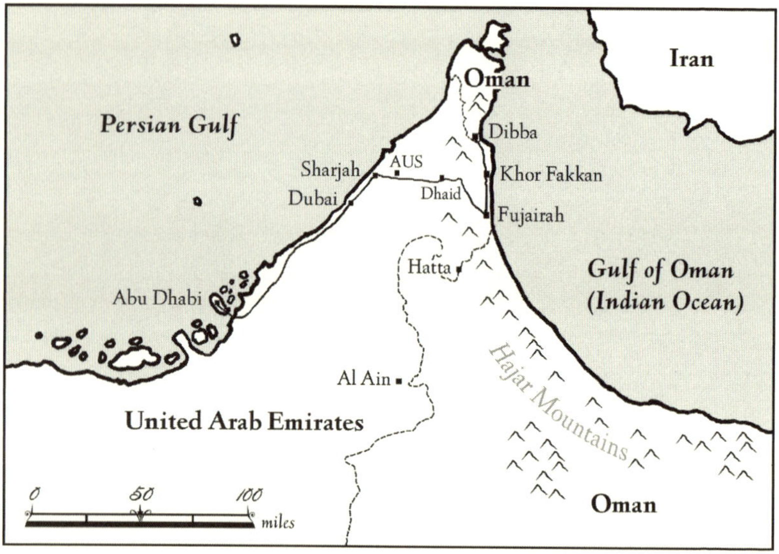

United Arab Emirates

Time and Space

Abayahs and Cell Phones

When I meet Americans in Internet chatrooms, I always have to explain that we don't live in tents and ride camels. Do they really think I'm sitting here on my camel writing to them?

—American University
of Sharjah freshman

I was about to land in Dubai and to begin my fourth stay in what my expatriate friends in Saudi Arabia used to call "the muddle east." I was coming to a familiar place—the Middle East—and to a new country—the United Arab Emirates. I was traveling into my own past—my memories of the six years I had spent in Egypt and Saudi Arabia during the 1980s—and my future. I had just signed a contract to teach for two years at the American University of Sharjah. I was also exploring internal times and spaces, and although I didn't know it then, I was going to a place that would seem to combine many places and times.

As I felt the plane begin its descent, however, I wondered what would go wrong this time and whom I would meet in the process. The third world, I thought, is the place where things never go as planned, but it is where I had always found people who were willing to help me out. I suppose this was because they too expected things to go wrong and didn't see any reason not to help if they could. A representative from the American University of Sharjah was supposed to meet me at the airport with my entry visa. Would he actually be there? A driver was supposed to meet me and take me to the university. Would he wait for the wrong flight and then go back without me, leaving me to try to find a taxi in the middle of the night? Most important, did the university really have faculty accommodations, as described in its brochure, or did the administration merely hope that there would be faculty housing in the future? Perhaps *stating* that housing existed was considered the first step toward making it so.

These worries were not as loony as they might sound. I remembered that once when I arrived in Saudi Arabia, the university where I was teaching had forgotten to send someone to meet me, and worse, had forgotten to assign housing to me, despite assurances that they would do both. And yet, I had not ended up wandering the streets with my suitcases as I had feared. One of my Arab colleagues, upon learning of my situation, came to collect me at the airport and let me stay with her and her family while the university administration arranged the housing they were supposed to have arranged in the first place.

Another time, flying back to Riyadh, Saudi Arabia, from London via Dhahran (on Saudi Arabia's east coast), I had learned halfway across the Mediterranean that (1) my flight to Riyadh was to leave from an airport 10 miles away from the airport where I would be landing in Dhahran, (2) there was no shuttle service between the two airports, and (3) it was dangerous for women traveling alone to take taxis. My travel agent and the airline had both neglected to inform me of this.

"No problem," the Saudi girl sitting next to me had said, examining my ticket. "My uncle lives in Dhahran and he is going to take me and my friends to the other airport anyway. You can come with us."

And thus I had found myself in the back of a big black Mercedes surrounded by a cheerful group of Saudi college girls, all delighted to have rescued a "doctora."

Such graciousness was overwhelming and more than a little humbling. Nevertheless, I was tired of being a sort of academic Blanche DuBois, always dependent on the kindness of strangers. While colorful adventures full of mishaps are great fun to tell to your friends back home, they are not what one wants at the time, at the end of a long trip. However, in the time and place in which I was landing—Dubai Airport in the summer of 1998—things actually worked.

Below me were lines of lights in the darkness, and then the wheels hit the runway. We were down. I gathered my belongings, said goodbye to the pleasant businessman sitting next to me, and headed for the main terminal. That was when something very odd happened. Nothing went wrong. Passport control sent me over to a desk that did not have a waiting line, and where a uniformed English-speaking Emirati promptly found my entry permit. My luggage was not lost. Still more surprising, given the fact that my flight was about four hours late, the university driver had waited for me. Soon I was being driven through the hot, humid September night down well-lit city streets lined with very American-looking shopping centers and strip malls. I could almost have been in a flight simulator for the past fourteen hours. Except for the heat, only the palm trees planted in the median and the absence of pedestrians let me know that I was no longer in Washington.

Then we were out of the city and into the desert. In the darkness, all I could see were the streetlights along the highway. After ten minutes or so, other shapes appeared out of the night, gas stations, grocery stores, garages, looking quiet and a little seedy (yes, I was in the third world after all). Suddenly, an arch that looked like the Arc de Triomphe straddled the highway and we were driving down a long, straight boulevard lined with domed buildings. Ahead was an imposing marble edifice with domes, arches, and columns, surrounded by formal gardens; this was the administration building, I learned later, but it looked like a mosque or a renaissance cathedral, and added to my feeling that I had traveled through a half dozen different countries and eras in the last twenty minutes. The driver circled around the building and pulled up in front of a two-story apartment building that would have been at home in the American southwest.

I overtipped the driver for carrying my heavy bags up the stairs, closed the door, and looked around. The place was small, but not cramped for one person, and obviously brand new. The furniture was also new, a generic motel modern that was at least inoffensive. The air conditioning and the refrigerator worked. Inside the fridge were a loaf of bread, a package of processed cheese, some apples, and a jar of instant coffee. Clean sheets had been laid out on the bed. Clearly, someone had been thinking ahead. The whole arrival seemed as if an idealized version of America had been transplanted into the Middle East, a sort of non-Adventureland where things worked and contingencies were anticipated. I put the thoughtfully arranged clean sheets on my bed and collapsed into a jag-lagged stupor.

The next day and in the weeks that followed, I tried to understand where I was. Still in that strange high that comes from mixing jet lag, excitement, disorientation, and culture shock, I began looking at maps of the Emirates, reading guidebooks, and exploring the city by bus and taxi. I quickly discovered that Sharjah and Dubai were growing so quickly that the inset city maps bore little relation to the actual layout of streets, but the map of the country was interesting as metaphor.

On the map, the UAE was a small country divided into what seemed like smaller countries. Each emirate had its own ruler, and the laws differed slightly from one emirate to the other. Some of the emirates were very rich; some were not. Some were very modern; some were not. And on the map, they were as oddly shaped and intertwined as gerrymandered voting precincts. Driving from Sharjah to the Indian Ocean coast, one could pass through three different emirates and a tiny piece of Oman and then wind up in Sharjah again on the other side. Added to this, each emirate included the traditional lands of various allied and competing tribes, although the word "tribe" in English suggests something far more primitive than the complex system of loyalties and social identities that defined what it meant to be tribal here.

Yet, while the map was a metaphor, there were other places that bordered one another even more strangely in ways that didn't show on the map. The independent and interlocking countries were not only Sharjah and Dubai and Abu Dhabi and all the other official emirates. The countries were also India, America, Russia, England, Lebanon, Syria, Iran, and France. There were more expatriate workers living in the Emirates than there were Emirati citizens. The average person in the Emirates was an Indian expatriate, not an Emirati. If the map could have shown cultures and peoples, the Emirates would have been an even tinier country than it is, with Europe, India, America, and the Levant all looming on its borders.

I had time to think about this a few weeks later, as I sat in a French-named coffee shop in an American-style shopping mall in Dubai drinking Italian espresso. A few tables away, a man in a *kandoora* (a traditional white robe, also called a *thobe* or a *dishdash*) was sipping coffee and speaking into a mobile phone. Two elegant Indian ladies in *salwar kamees* cooed over a fussy toddler in a stroller while they ate French pastries. And around us strolled the shoppers. Women in the traditional *abayahs* (veils) and *burqas* (the beaked masks with cutouts for eyes) stood veil to bare bicep with Eastern European tourists in miniskirts and halter tops, all looking at the same massive gold necklaces in the windows of the jewelry shops. Packs of teenage Arab girls, some in *abayahs* and *shillahs* (headscarves), some in skin-tight spandex and cropped tops, whispered and giggled. (I wondered if some of the girls in the sexy outfits had left their houses in *abayahs* and then stuffed the veils in their purses as soon as they got to the mall.) Their male counterparts were sometimes in jeans, sometimes in *kandooras*, but in the latter case the traditional *ghutra* and *agal* had been replaced by the ubiquitous backwards baseball cab. What did their attire mean? That their bodies were in the traditional Arab world but that their heads were in American pop culture? The symbolism did not augur well.

But perhaps that was too glib. The mall itself was an American-style monument to consumerism, the sort of many-storied, escalatored, sky-lighted palace that one would find in any affluent American suburb. The people were different—they were Arabs, Indians, and Europeans. The stores were different—there were no big, upscale department stores anchoring either end, and gold and oriental carpet stores outnumbered the women's clothing shops by far. Yet the most important difference was that the atmosphere was far more cosmopolitan than anything I had seen in the States—or indeed anyplace else. In America, the veiled women would have been stared at, and bold strangers might even have asked them why they were dressed so strangely. (A Saudi woman I knew in Pennsylvania had grown so exasperated by this question that she started telling people that she was going to a Halloween party, no matter what the season.) A few hundred miles away, in Saudi Arabia, I was leered at on the streets even when I was wearing an *abayah*, and old men shouted "Cover yourself, woman" (in Arabic, but I understood) if I went out without a head-scarf. Here, no one seemed to care how other people dressed. As I was thinking this, two pretty young blondes in tight jeans walked by the café, and the men drinking coffee continued to talk on their cell phones or read their newspapers. If they noticed and appreciated, they noticed and appreciated discretely. If they disapproved, they kept their disapproval to themselves.

"The Gulf" and "the Arab world," I decided, are very misleading terms, implying as they do that all the Arab countries share a common culture. It has some basis in fact, but it is a very incomplete truth. On a level of high culture—literature and religion—all Arab countries do share a common culture.

And many of the underlying social structures are the same: the extended family and the networks of exchange of favors, for instance. And yet, manners and outlooks differ vastly, including the outlook toward foreigners and foreign cultures and new ideas. In the Emirates, unlike so many other places I had lived, people seem willing to accept elements of other cultures without feeling threatened by what was new and different, at least concerning external things.

I could see this tolerance and eclecticism to some degree in the dress of my students. The way people dress is usually a clue to their identities, whether or not they consciously decide to make a "fashion statement." But here were a dozen different contradictory statements. Some of the girls wore strapless tops and jeans. Some wore *abayahs* and *shillahs* but left a bit of their hair showing in front. Some covered every lock. Some wore head-coverings and jeans, and others wore *abayahs* but left their hair uncovered. Some of the boys from the Gulf countries always wore *kandooras*, but others would wear jeans one day and a kandoora the next. If the clothing spoke about the wearers, it seemed to be saying, "I'm Western, I'm Arab, I'm a good Muslim, I'm traditional, I want to be noticed, I'm fashionable, and look at what a good figure I have," sometimes all at once. If the clothes were any clue to cultural identity, they seemed to suggest that various cultural identities were acceptable and even that cultural identity itself could be changed according to circumstance and mood. Costumes and clothing were interchangeable.

And stranger still than the styles were ways in which time periods seemed to border one another. Although the technology my students used was that of the twenty-first century, the customs and tools of the sixteenth century were still within living memory. Fifty years ago, it had been safer and easier to travel by camel than by car because there were so few roads. Men dived for pearls without any breathing devices from dhows whose basic designs hadn't changed for a thousand years. Now, most of the students had mobile phones. They loved fast cars and jet-skis and dune buggies and powerboats and, indeed, any technology related to communications or speed. The country had gone from being preindustrial and premodern to postindustrial and postmodern without ever having been industrial and modern.

In one sense, the adoption of Western fashion and technology was superficial. Students could carry cell phones and wear baseball caps without feeling that their culture was threatened because of the strong sense of identity that came from family, religion, and tribe. And yet the tolerance of other values was not superficial. Christians and Hindus were free to practice their religion openly. In Saudi Arabia, Christians had been deported for forming home prayer groups, and even in a more open society like Egypt, the indigenous Coptic Christians were not allowed to build or repair churches without government permission, which meant that many churches were nearly ruins. Here in the Emirates, my Mormon friend regularly attended services in Dubai, and another friend went to the Catholic church in Sharjah. The English language newspapers ran accounts of all the Hindu festivals and pictures of the celebrations. On Hindu and Muslim feast days, students went around distributing candy to all their friends and teachers, regardless of their religion. Of course, exchanging candy is very different from exchanging opinions, and I never heard any real religious debate, but tolerance and respect do not necessarily require full understanding. The tolerance in itself was remarkable.

I often wondered what this meant, and why so many seemingly jarring and conflicting attitudes and assumptions, so many times and places, could exist at once, within the same people. I could come up with only tentative answers, knowing that the answers came out of my own impatience with confusion and my desire to like where I had come. I could say that one reason lay in the geography and history of the Emirates themselves. Contact with other cultures and other technologies was nothing new here. The Emiratis had always looked to the sea that connected them to other places and cultures, not to the deserts that separated them from the rest of the world. There had been contact with Persia since the Bronze Age; the ancient Persians had introduced the whole system of mountain wells and aqueducts that transformed valleys into oases. There had been trade with India and China since the Middle Ages; archeologists have found the lovely high-fired Chinese blue porcelain of the Sung Dynasty in digs hundreds of miles inland. And of course there had been contact with the West, primarily with the British, in the eighteenth, nineteenth, and twentieth centuries. The current relationship with America and the West might be somewhat uncomfortable politically, but it seemed to be very profitable economically.

In the Emirates I didn't find the sort of love/hate stance toward the West that I had thought was characteristic of the Arab world. It was more of a polite and detached interest, like the men in the café when the girls in jeans walked by. The tolerance, the eclecticism, and the efficiency were all part of the same worldview. If something worked, the Emiratis adopted it. If other people did things they didn't approve of, the Emiratis ignored them. The outlook was not necessarily intellectually sophisticated—because for many people the contact had been with objects and behaviors, not ideas and values—but it was certainly worldly and cosmopolitan. The muddle east I thought I would find seemed to be a kind of melded east, I suppose, where times and places could blend—at least at this time, in this place.

Sharjah and Dubai

Cities on the Sand

Safe upon the solid rock the ugly houses stand
Come and see my shining castles built upon the sand.

—Edna St. Vincent Millay

During my first semester in the Emirates, I spent as much of my spare time as I could in Sharjah and Dubai, the two nearest cities. I walked around, I shopped, and I looked at people, trying to get a sense of these places and trying to listen to what they had to say to me.

A place is always in a dialogue with the perceiver. There will always be something missing, ellipses in the description, pieces left out of the collage, gaps that the mind fills in for itself. In these gaps resides the spirit of the place, which only the mental eye can see. Sharjah and Dubai are real cities, but Sharjah and Dubai are also imaginary cities, not only to me, but to everyone who sees and tries to understand this or any other place.

My plane landed in Dubai. I shopped in Dubai and went to movies and restaurants in Dubai. But I lived and worked in Sharjah. "Sharjah," an Emirati friend said to me, "is the New

Jersey of Dubai." And when I first arrived, I thought of Sharjah as the younger sister of the beauty queen Dubai, a younger sister that wasn't bad looking but still had a few pimples and a retaining wire on her teeth. But both metaphors are true only in the way that a bad photograph is true: it's what both cities do look like now, at this moment in time, but the photos don't show the moment before or the moment later, when both could look very different. And like bad pictures, these metaphors don't show the spirit. To understand what Sharjah and Dubai look like and feel like, one needs pictures from different angles, from different times, and one needs to realize that these pictures will not reveal important intangible things about a place. The history, the hopes for the future, the values that arise and erode like the buildings can only be sensed and imagined.

Dubai and Sharjah were already enshrined in "now" and "then" photos, with "then" shots of both taken from the air in the late sixties, just before independence, when they looked to be little more than clusters of buildings along each side of their harbors. These photos are always contrasted with the "now" shots of modern, sprawling cities. Sharjah and Dubai, and perhaps most of southern Arabia, have prospered since they gained independence, and not just because they had oil, since these two particular emirates don't have very much. They thrived, I think, because the Emirati government has done a better job of running the country than the British-controlled government did. And more than that, self-government has fostered hope and pride.

Dubai

Dubai is a city in the sky, a city of wealth and beauty and courtesy, with its still-wealthier future hovering above it like a mirage. It is also a city on the sand, build on the inequalities and distortions and exploitations that arose in the past and continue into the present.

Nevertheless, the old photo of Dubai is misleading, because at the time of the picture, Dubai was already a thriving trading center and had been for almost a century. It had been the center of the pearl trade during the early part of the century, for one thing, and thus had a fairly wealthy merchant class, although many of these wealthy merchants were not Emiratis. Most of the local people were poor, but the city itself was not. Because it had a deep-water port, it had also been a redistribution center for British goods bound for India, Iran, and Iraq. Under British "protection," British companies had established businesses and had begun importing low-wage laborers from India to build factories and offices and housing. All of this gave Dubai the basis for what it became in the "now" shots, a city that extended for miles along the coast of the Arabian Gulf, surrounded by rings of suburban housing developments pushing further and further into the desert. And now the local people were relatively rich, and the relatively poor were the Indian and Iranian laborers and the Indonesian housemaids, whose cheap labor had continued to make the city so attractive to investors. The Emiratis didn't start this system of immigrant labor, and it was certainly a morally ambiguous arrangement, but it was hard to know how to stop this system without destroying the dream city that was built on it.

Perhaps this inequality was part of the reason that the government was re-creating a simpler past for public consumption, one that was not false but which left out all that was troubling. The past that had been preserved was not the past that underlay the prosperity or the inequality, but was an apolitical past of nineteenth-century life along the waterfront "heritage area" and "heritage village," with models of Bedouin houses, fishermen's huts, and oasis farmhouses. The heritage villages were tasteful and informative and filled with Emirati and Indian families who wanted their children to see how their grandparents lived or who simply wanted an "educational" family outing. The children climbed around on models of dhows and peered excitedly into traditional kitchens, where women prepared Arabic flat bread on big stone griddles and sold it fresh to visitors. Like Mount Vernon or Williamsburg for American children, the villages recreated a past that was a delightful game. This depiction was all very well-intentioned and was much better than letting the past disappear. But this past didn't seem solid enough, or true enough, to build a city on. The city wasn't rooted in this past because most of the people in Dubai are from somewhere else. It isn't their past. The buildings and streets where people lived and worked were all new. Dubai's past was a curiosity for them, not an identity.

Driving around Dubai as it is now, it was easy to get the impression that everything was new and everyone was rich. Part of this impression came from the architecture; it sometimes seemed as if potential building investors had given several young architects blank checks and told them, "Build me something astonishing," and the architects did. Not necessarily astonishingly good, but certainly astonishing. So there were hotels that looked like sailboats and yacht clubs that looked like the Sydney Opera House and shopping malls that looked like pink castles. There were spherical buildings made out of mirror glass and pencil-shaped buildings topped with spheres. Dubai had a Planet Hollywood, but it really would be far more appropriate for Hollywood to have a Planet Dubai. The newness and the foreignness of the buildings were an emblem of Dubai at its best and its worst.

Dubai was not quite a Western city, despite its Western architecture. In a way, Dubai made a great many European and American cities look shabby. Dubai was very, very rich because it was a major center for the reshipment of goods between Europe and Asia, and because it was an important banking center. In this respect, it was a bit like Hong Kong or Zurich. Dubai expanded into an embodiment of the late twentieth century, the way Florence did in the fourteenth century and Paris in the nineteenth, but the analogy isn't exact. Dubai didn't have the international political power that Florence and Paris once did, and wealth without power creates vulnerability.

Perhaps this vulnerability was the sand that underlay Dubai's frantic consumer culture. Because the majority of people in Dubai were foreigners who would eventually go back to their own countries, they had no real commitment to the society. They came to work and to buy things to take back home with them.

"It's nothing but people buying and selling and being discontent with what they have because someone else has something more expensive," a French Moroccan student told me. "The Europeans and Westernized Arab kids spend their days at the beach and their nights in the clubs, and the non-

Westernized Arab kids spend their days and nights watching video movies of other people going to beaches and bars. And nobody has more of an idea in his head than the day he was born," she said, sitting across from my desk and looking like cartoon of rebellious sexuality in her low-cut tank top and her tight jeans. I liked her anyway. She had written excellent papers in my class and her clothes seemed just a way of stating to the world that she was not local. I ventured that perhaps part of the reason for this consumerism was that the wealth was relatively new here, but she just shrugged. "I think it's becoming the same everywhere," she said. "It's part of an international greediness movement."

Although they came from a different tradition, many of the Islamists in the region made very similar criticisms, seeing the consumerism as Western values tempting people away from their responsibilities toward God and their fellow man. I recalled reading a Saudi Shiite imam who suggested that consumerism was a kind of addiction through which the West kept the Arab world dependent on its products and thus open to policies contrary to Arab interests. Some of my students saw the preoccupation with wealth as a more secular lapse, but also the result of Western influence. "Nobody cares about friendship anymore," one student told me. "All people want to know you for is to make business contacts. We've forgotten our Arab values."

Sometimes Dubai seemed to be a kind of timeless fantasy world, like Las Vegas, except that instead of the timeless unreality of gambling casinos, Dubai was the timeless unreality of shopping malls. The feeling is the same. Money doesn't matter. Work doesn't matter. The object is to play the game well and be a winner, and in this case, being a winner means owning expensive things. This kind of attitude was hardly unique to Dubai. And yet here, it did seem to have a different form, if only because there was so much money and so little to contradict money's loud and insistent voice.

Sometimes, wandering through these mirrored malls, I would see my reflection and not recognize myself; I would think, for an instant, "That woman looks like me, only older." And then I would realize that she was I. Looking at Dubai, I often saw distorted values, and then realized, with a shock, that these were American values as well. I thought of this as I stood in a jewelry store once (yes, I succumb to the glamour, too) watching a woman buying a heavy gold necklace for a seven—or eight-year-old child. "Wouldn't a little girl that age really rather have a bike or a game, something she could play with?" I thought, and then I looked at the child's entranced face and shining eyes and realized, "No, she wouldn't. She really does want a six-hundred-dollar necklace." For many foreign workers in Dubai, six hundred dollars would be several months' wages. Dubai seemed to have so much wealth, so much poverty, and so few people troubled by the disparity.

In America, the same disparities in wealth that I found so offensive here were smoothed over by the pretense that everyone was middle class and equal. In the Emirates, the poor deferred to me, called me "madam," and offered to clean my house, wash my car, or carry my groceries for whatever spare change I was willing to give. Whether they were janitors, salespeople, hairdressers, or gardeners, I couldn't forget that they made much less money than I did because they treated me as if I were the lady of the manor and they were the servants. In America, the checkout clerk or the janitor was just a person doing a job, my equal. Yet, if he didn't need to defer to me, I didn't need to think about the difference in our incomes or worry about how he was getting by. The slums and migrant laborers' camps were out of my line of vision at home, and habit had blinded me to social ills that the newness and otherness of Dubai made so visible. In America, construction workers didn't sleep under their trucks at night beside the palatial homes they were building, but homeless people still slept in the streets, I realized. In that instant, Dubai became a mirror in which I saw America.

In Dubai, the poor were usually foreign, which made their poverty easy to accept. It can be difficult under the best of circumstances for the rich to feel much compassion for the poor, but if they are from a different country and culture, it becomes more difficult still. It becomes easy to think that the poor are living in poverty because they are inferior, not because they are unlucky, and it is easy to assume an unearned superiority when one is treated as a superior. Not everyone made these assumptions, but it was much easier not to question. This failure to think was at the heart of the moral malaise that both westerners and easterners sensed in Dubai.

Then I looked in the mirror again at America and wondered if the reasons that we tolerate poverty were the same. Foreign migrant laborers in the United States weren't much better off than those in the UAE; there were just fewer of them. And those of our poor who weren't literally foreign were minorities or transformed into minorities: welfare queens and trailer-park trash. Not us. Who cares? The situations and their causes were not precisely the same, but the parallels should caution against smugness.

And yet, the very sand on which Dubai was built was

beautiful, both in the literal sand of its lovely public beaches and in the metaphorical sense of its uneasy foundation on foreign commerce and influence. Even when the sand was a metaphor for Dubai's political vulnerability and its inequalities, the city on the sand and all that city embodied created a place of the mind where ideas and values could blend and transform. International commerce and wealth had brought freedom, and at times East and West seemed to have blended into a perfect hybrid. In Dubai's international spaces, men and women could redefine themselves. On the beaches themselves, westerners and Indians and Arabs mingled without intruding into one another's worlds. The boundaries were permeable as the sand.

In other public spaces, like the sidewalk cafés along tree-lined Daiyafa Street, local women could have coffee with their friends without risking their reputations, and I could spend hours strolling and sitting and watching people. Indians ran the Indian restaurants and Italians ran Italian restaurants, without making the spices less subtle to appeal to mass taste as they often do in the United States. I could feel, for a moment, that I was in India or Italy, except that everything was so gleaming and new. In Dubai, I could pretend to be almost anywhere else. I could disappear into a totally Western space for a moment, have a glass of wine and a sandwich in the yacht club, and watch the lights of the cruise boats as they make their circuit of Dubai's lagoon. I could go to one of the many English language bookstores, where my fellow-shoppers were as likely to be Indians or Arabs as Western expats. I could sit in the vine-covered arbor of the bookstore's café and read and watch people from all over the world doing the same thing.

No one bothered anyone. In Egypt or Saudi Arabia, taxi drivers and merchants would lecture me about the unfairness of American foreign policy. And yet, in a way, while the freedom and anonymity were relaxing, the absence of the political and the personal made these spaces seem cut off from their surroundings. It sometimes felt as if all the rough edges that make an Arab city real had been rubbed off to make Dubai more comfortable for expats; for foreigners in Dubai, everyone was foreign and no one cared what other people did. People could select their places, try on temporary identities, question values, become something new.

Around all this foreignness, the Emiratis of Dubai lived their lives with a freedom that a monocultural society might not permit. One March afternoon, I was sitting on a deserted part of the beach where my friends and I could sunbathe without becoming a spectacle. Most of the Arab families used other sections of the beach, perhaps because they didn't particularly want to mix with Western women in bathing suits. I was gazing out to sea when I saw a young Arab woman in an *abayah* striding confidently along the water's edge, a book in her hand, her face serious but not sad. The wind blew the *abayah* open, revealing loose pants rolled up to the knee. The girl was enjoying the beauty of the sand and the water, and she could do this here because it was a neutral space, a foreign space, where no one would assume that she was out alone in order to attract men. She could wear the clothing that made her feel modest and dignified, but she was free to go where she chose. Feeling me watching her, she nodded a greeting and continued on toward the jagged rocks at the beach's end.

Sharjah

Sharjah would seem to be a very pleasant little city if Dubai weren't just ten miles away, inviting invidious comparisons. It too had recently prospered and had at least some of the glow that comes from things having gone right. It had miles of lovely wide public beaches, although the beaches were a bit littered, and only men and children went in the water. The women stayed fully clothed, in the shade, because Sharjah was more conservative than Dubai and had fewer westerners to set a flagrant example. If Dubai was a hybrid of East and West, Sharjah blended the Arab world with Iran and the Subcontinent, with fewer hints of the West. I saw no solitary women striding past bikinied foreigners along the Sharjah beaches; but I did see little groups of Arab girls in *abayahs* and Indian girls in *salwar kamees* strolling by the sea wall in the evening, enjoying the night air, the exercise, and each other's company.

Sharjah was a little dusty, a bit low key, a bit languid (except when you were trying to brave the traffic), and this slower-paced ambiance was pleasant. It seemed to lack the extremes of wealth and poverty that were so blatant in Dubai, and although this was an illusion to a degree (the workers' barracks and the palaces were both out of sight, in the city's outskirts), the illusion prevented one from feeling troubled. Unlike Dubai, Sharjah could seem like a backdrop of unthreatening differentness. Yet Sharjah was also a city on the sand, vulnerable, contradictory, illusive, never quite what it seemed.

Sharjah did not feel rich and new. With the exception of a few new skyscrapers of the glass-pencils-balancing-geometrical-shapes variety, most of the buildings seemed to be no more than five or six stories high, white or light brown, and at least a few decades old. In fact, many of its museums and public building were much newer than that, but builders have tended to favor more traditional architecture. Domes and columns abound. From a car window, at least, it looked like what it was, a small and relatively prosperous Arab city.

When explored on foot, Sharjah was a slightly different city than it seemed from a car—colorful, varied, even friendly in a timid and respectful way. And on foot you could discover that it was also not precisely an Arab city either, since almost all the merchants and salespeople were Asian. There were some Emiratis among the peoples of Sharjah, but they were not very obvious.

I discovered this as I walked along Sharjah's small working harbor, where shallow-draft fishing and trading dhows unload their wares to sell in the nearby open-air souks. Along one part of the lagoon is a kind of boardwalk with hotels, restaurants, and a few high-rise apartment buildings, but further down are souks and the docks. On one end is the modern world, posh and anonymous, and on the other is a glimpse of the past. As I walked along this past, the air smelled of sun and salt water and faintly of fish from the fish souk further along the lagoon; the sun sparkled on the gently rippling water, and a seagull squawked.

Nobody seemed to be in much of a hurry, which made me feel freer to nose around and explore. A few men fished from the corniche, mostly Indians in clean but mismatched Western-style clothes, probably laborers from the construction sites who had the day off. Further along, men sat crossed-legged on the heavy wooden dhows, smoking and watching the passersby with mild interest. Most of them wore turbans and colored *kandooras*, but I wasn't sure if they were Emirati because they looked so different from the spotlessly white-clad Emirati businessmen I had seen in Dubai.

I looked at the heaped-up boxes on the wharf for a clue and found that most of them contained either fresh fruits or vegetables or, strangely, small appliances and kitchen goods. I suppose that the dhows were bringing in produce from the northern emirates, which received enough of the monsoon rains for agriculture, and then taking back manufactured goods imported into Sharjah to resell at smaller and shabbier dockside souks in the coastal fishing villages. These were working class Emiratis, the seagoing version of independent truckers. Seeing me looking at the cargo, one of the sailors greeted me and asked me where I was from, which gave me the chance to ask him where he was from. Ras-Al-Khaimah, he told me, naming a northern emirate. My guess had been right. I walked on, and he went back to his conversation with a shipmate.

A hundred years ago, this area along the lagoon and a short strip of coast were all there was of Sharjah. Less than a mile away, there was a big medieval-looking fort dating from the early nineteenth century, and a little further inland was a nineteenth-century merchant's house that had been restored as a museum. Sharjah felt connected to its past; this too was in part an illusion.

It would be easy to think that Sharjah was just a nineteenth-century fishing village, with no particular history or culture, that gradually grew into a city with the coming of the oil wealth, and in fact that is what many of the expatriates do think. I've heard old Brits reminisce about the sixties, when

Sharjah was nothing but an airstrip and a few huts made out of palm fronds. In the last fifty years, Sharjah had gone from being very poor to being comfortably well off. And yet, if one looks at centuries instead of decades, Sharjah's history tells a very different story.

Sharjah was once a beautiful and wealthy city, one of the main trading ports on the Arabian Gulf. In the sixteenth and seventeenth centuries, Sharjah was the big city, and Dubai the backwater. There are no old photographs to show this, only merchants' records and travelers' accounts, and histories based on these records, and this history seldom appears in Western textbooks. But scholars of the Indian Ocean and Arabian Gulf maritime trade have written about what Sharjah was and what happened to change all that. The Portuguese, the Dutch, and finally the British took over these trade routes and the countries with which Sharjah traded; Sharjah was marginalized.

Then, in the early nineteenth century, the local sheikhs were able to re-establish a large commercial fleet and controlled much of the commerce in the Gulf, while the British, who had taken over the Indian Ocean trade (and much of India as well), were busy fighting Napoleon. But when that conflict was over, the British turned their attention to the growing threat that southeastern Arabia might become both wealthy and politically united enough to endanger their influence in the region. Saying they were eliminating piracy (a very controversial claim), the British destroyed the local commercial fleet. After that, the only native vessels allowed to sail were fishing and pearling boats. Sharjah and the northern emirates were effectively cut off from the outside world for almost a hundred years.

Sharjah was growing too fast and becoming too wealthy to keep its current ambiance much longer. Sharjah's future was already evident on the outskirts of the city, where the Sharjah government had established free trade zones for foreign companies to build factories tax-free. Although this arrangement contributed to the local economy, it was a questionable foundation for prosperity. The workers were imported, and the Western companies that built here didn't have to comply with their own countries' labor and environmental laws. Yet on these same salt flats the government had also built universities that were growing like mushrooms. In fact, with all their domes, they looked like clumps of mushrooms, too. The students and faculty could smell the gases from the factories, and the factory workers were driven past the landscaped gardens of the universities in big open trucks. Often on weekends, I would see these workers taking pictures of one another in front of the massive marble gate, perhaps hoping to convince their families back home that they are a part of all that the gardens and domes imply.

Hope radiates from both Sharjah and Dubai, as palpable as the heat, more precious than the oil and pearls, and just as vulnerable. Decades or centuries from now, both cities may disappear into the sand, for no one can predict the shifts of history. The images and all they say and don't say will be scattered throughout the world.

Hatta

Off the Beaten Track of History

Yet all experience is an arch wherethrough
Gleams that untraveled world whose margins fade
Forever and forever as I move

—Tennyson

After I began to have a sense of Sharjah and Dubai as physical places and places of my own imagination, I started to long for more. I couldn't find what lay within the cities, not yet, because I didn't know the societies well enough, but I could find what lay beyond them, or at least in the landscapes that surrounded them. When the weather started to cool, I began to explore the countryside, trying to find places off the beaten track.

Thus I found myself standing at the gate of the watch-tower in the inland oasis town of Hatta, looking out over the jagged foothills of the Hajar Mountains. Row after row of increasingly steep and barren mountains rose in the distance, the last range so high and so dim that I was not sure if I was seeing the outlines of mountains or low gray clouds. Those mountains were in Oman, another country. Below me was

Hatta, its outlying farms and fields improbably green with clover against the more subdued green of the orange trees and date palms. How stunning it must have been for desert travelers in the past to trudge through miles and miles of red sand dunes and then, suddenly, find all this green. I felt as if I were at the ends of the earth. It was so romantic, so exotic, so lovely.

A hundred years earlier, three hundred years earlier, even a thousand years earlier, men had stood on watchtowers like this one, looking for—what? Caravans coming in from the desert that would use this oasis as a watering place before continuing across the narrow peninsula that separated the Arabian Gulf from the Indian Ocean? Or were they looking out for raiding tribesmen coming in from the mountains and desert to steal livestock? Whichever it was, I forced myself to realize they hadn't stood on this particular tower. The tower where I stood was a restoration, part of a "heritage village" funded by the Dubai government. The village, a sort of outdoor museum, wasn't open yet, so it felt as empty and deserted as an "authentic" historical site. And since the tower was on one of the two hills that loomed above the town, there had probably once been a watchtower here. The foundations looked old—the stones massive, weathered, and hand chiseled. There certainly had been a watchtower system, and there were hundreds of unrestored watchtowers throughout the Emirates and Oman.

Fifty years earlier, this tower had probably been just its foundation stones. Then, in the late 1990s, the Dubai government realized the importance of the outward symbols of history, archeologists and historians studied how the old towers had been made, and workmen using this knowledge put this tower back together again. The tower might have been accurate historically, but it was an interpreted history. History aboveground is often an interpreted history. After all, even the aboveground history in history books is a tower built out of the foundation stones of primary sources. And it seems to me that, although these historical towers might be perfectly sound structures too, it's still hard to know how the towers looked to the people who used them or how the history felt to the people who lived it.

The history that existed under the ground was perhaps more authentic. Two thousand years ago, the people living in this part of the Emirates had devised a falaj system of mountain wells and aqueducts that brought water from underground aquifers down into this valley. The system itself was a masterpiece of ancient technology at least as sophisticated as that of the Romans, and it probably predated them. Over the years, this irrigation system had been destroyed and rebuilt many times, and these wells were what made Hatta an oasis. The system was still in use, although new pipes replaced the older ones and the system itself was now augmented with water from other sources. Underground history doesn't freeze a moment in time; time and objects in time keep flowing and changing. Underground history is a record of changes continuing into the present, subtle and unseen.

What I saw now, I saw through my own romantic imagination; I could see caravans and tribal raiders if I wanted to, and I would not be entirely wrong, but this was a reconstruction as much as the tower. The only difference was that it was my own interpretation, or misinterpretation, not someone else's. I saw what I wanted to see, and one thing I wanted to see were vestiges of a time both more primitive and more exciting than my own. That's part of the fascination of history.

Yet I saw many things that day that made me wonder exactly what words like "authentic" and "historical" meant, and what it meant to be so far away from a history I had learned.

Here, I wanted everything to be "authentic," to be just as it was. If I had been walking around the Gettysburg battlefield, I don't think it would have occurred to me to wonder if what I saw was exactly what the battlefield looked like in 1863. Although the battlefield park was an interpretation of history, too, the place would have felt "historical" to me because it was part of a history I had learned in grade school, and learning it was part of my earliest memories. National history and personal history intertwined to make that past real. Here, where I had to rely on recently learned and simplified history, I wanted every stone to be the same.

Earlier that day I had made the trip through the dunes myself, not in a camel caravan, but in an SUV, along with two friends from the English department. Although a four-lane highway could have taken us more directly from Dubai to Hatta, we had decided to take advantage of the four-wheel-drive option and to drive through a wadi, a dry river bed that stretched from just a few miles outside of Sharjah all the way to these mountains. The wadi was well known and well traveled, and in fact we saw one or two other cars along the way, but it still felt like an adventure.

As soon as we left the university compound, the topography changed. We moved from salt flats to beige sand dunes to the red sand that comprises most of the central peninsula. The carefully transplanted and watered palm trees of the campus (often with their tops still wrapped in burlap bags to protect the hearts until the roots took hold) gave way to eucalyptus and acacia imported from Australia at the beginning of the twentieth century, and then to still stranger native plants called Sodom's apples (a gray-green cactus-like shrub) and ghuff trees, which grew along the banks of the wadi and looked like willows. Camels and goats grazed on the sparse vegetation. Every four or five miles, we would come across a small town, usually just a gas station, a mosque, and a couple of dingy-looking stores. The urban and urbane world of Dubai was behind us, at least on the outside.

And then, as soon as we turned off the road into the wadi itself, there was nothing but sand and rock for miles, with the bare mountains towering in the distance. The car slithered and carved deep ruts into the sand, but we kept moving forward. It felt like driving on ice, but if we had driven any more slowly, we would have risked getting stuck. As it was, we were lucky that other four-wheel-drive vehicles had packed the sand down for us.

About half way along the wadi, we decided to stop the car and climb one of the dunes. The desert was shockingly silent after hours of listening to our own conversation and the noise of the motor. At first, there seemed to be no sound at all. Then, gradually, we could hear a few birdcalls. Nothing else.

From the top of the dune, we could see a tiny settlement, perhaps just one or two houses, among a grove of date palms. An underground spring must have come to the surface here, giving enough water for the traditional subsistence farming based on dates and goats. What interested us more at first, however, were two semicircular stone walls built along the side of the dune. They looked like snipers' nests, and sure enough, we found spent shells in the sand next to each one. I imagined tribal warfare, with men in Lawrence of Arabia costumes attacking the farm below. Later, one of my students suggested the gunmen were probably the farmers themselves, shooting feral dogs that were attacking their livestock.

The reality of what life had been like in the emirates and what it continued to be for many people was probably the life that was being lived now in that farmhouse. Clearly, life here was still harsh, but not in a dramatic or exciting way. They didn't have to contend with tribal raids, but getting enough water year round couldn't have been easy. The drive to the main highway would seem long, especially if someone were sick or injured. The farmers might have electricity and air conditioning, but they didn't have the desalinated water or the trade or the contact with the outside world that made Dubai a modern city. In fifty or so miles, we had traveled a hundred years and were now on another, earlier planet. As I watched, a figure moved out of one of the houses—a woman, I guessed, from the brightly colored clothes—and disappeared into the grove of date palms.

"What would it be like to live in that house down there," I wondered. The woman probably lived not very differently from her parents and grandparents, except for the imported technology. I could only imagine a hard and lonely life, cooking, tending children, perhaps going outside only to look after livestock. There might be compensations: a warm family life, some contact with the outside world through watching television and listening to music, surely visits from relatives. It would be no worse than most women's lives throughout human history, and it would be better than some, but I couldn't imagine how I could have lived a life like that—at least not and be anyone I would recognize as myself. And I suppose that to the women of this household, my life would seem romantic and exotic, something out of a television program.

I was on the outside of this way of life. I could only look at it and imagine and then get back into the car again. As we closed the car doors and drove out of sight of the farmhouse, the scene changed again to desert and rock and emptiness.

The outside scene changed again as we drove into Hatta. Hatta, I was told, was remote and unspoiled; that was why we had come there, to see a way of life that was different from that of the coastal cities. And yet, after the desert and that isolated farmhouse, it felt like a return to civilization. The houses followed traditional Arab architecture, but this style is now common in modern houses in warm climates throughout the world: flat roofs, thick stucco walls, small exterior windows, all surrounded by a privacy wall. The stores and gas stations where we stopped to ask directions were not quite as large or well stocked as the supermarkets in Dubai, but they were certainly adequate. Even the fact that part of the village had been restored and turned into a museum made it seem modern because it made the recent past seem so much longer ago.

Was I or was I not off the beaten track? Quite literally, I had been on the beaten track, or I would have been stuck in the sand. And now, as I looked at the town below the watchtower, the pleasant-looking houses, satellite dishes, stations, and minimarts, could almost have been along an interstate highway in Utah or Nevada.

Yet *almost* is still the operative word here. As the sun set over the last mountain range and the clouds above the horizon turned pink in a salmon-colored sky, the muezzin began to call the evening prayer. The watchtower on which I stood evoked a different history than the history of America, a history no less real for being an interpretation. It said that this place was not just what it is; it was what it had been. Its history was a part of it, both below the surface in the falaj and as a shaping force. I could only see the place and the history through my own imagination and my desire to be where someone of another time had lived a life more exciting than my own. But if my imagination was a filter, what was outside the filter maintained its own identity, to be seen and interpreted and reinterpreted by everyone who came to this place.

Forty years ago, when British travel writer Wilfred Thesiger (*Arabian Sands*) traveled by camel across the Wahiba Sands of the Empty Quarter to Oman and the Trucial States (as the emirates were then called), towns like Hatta and Al Ain seemed impossibly exotic and romantic, in part because they were almost inaccessible to westerners. One reached Hatta by camel caravan or by jeep; the latter was far more risky because there were so few paved roads. Today anyone can fly into Dubai, drive to Hatta, and stay overnight in a luxury hotel. It's become harder and harder to feel like an explorer, if being an explorer means danger and discomfort. And yet, here I was in a beautiful place that no one I knew at home had ever heard of, looking at a thousand years of history that had not been taught in any American schoolbook.

We got back into the car and drove to the hotel for dinner, a lovely hotel with beautifully landscaped grounds, multiple swimming pools, a golf course, skeet shooting, and a landing pad for helicopters. But there was something jarring about it still. In the lobby, the management had set up a model of a Bedouin tent with real hand-woven tribal rugs on the floor and female mannequins in veils and *burqas* making coffee over a plastic fire while a male mannequin cleaned an antique rifle. It looked like one of the dioramas in the Smithsonian.

There was something very disquieting about this display in a way that the restored watchtower was not. It wasn't that it was badly done. The brass coffee urns and the antique guns and the weaving all looked authentic. Nor was the impulse behind the display solely commercial. Indeed, it seemed essentially educational, to show the Western hotel guests how people in the Emirates had once lived and to give a sense of place. And yet it was disturbing, for reasons I didn't realize until about an hour later.

We were sitting in the hotel bar over dinner and drinks, while at the bar, a group of clean-cut, earnestly engaged, rather red-faced, and slightly drunken young men (South African engineers, we guessed, based on what we could pick up from their accents and conversation) slapped each other on the back and told jokes. The bar itself was a replica of a British pub, all polished wood and brass, with comfortable chairs inviting a long stay and dart boards and reproductions of Stubbs horses on the walls evoking ye olde England, although my English friend told me that the pub was more a colonial's nostalgic vision of England than any England he remembered. We were inside an interpretation, he suggested.

I suppose it was the sudden awareness that I was in a replica myself that made me realize what I didn't like about the replica of the Bedouin household. For a moment, I could imagine the bar scene turned into a diorama, with mannequins in Gap sportswear sitting at the real oak tables with plastic beers and plates of fish and chips in front of them. I imagined the local women I had seen a few hours earlier coming to peer at the scene and remark on our oddness. The image made me laugh at first, but it implied an idea more sobering. After all, the people depicted in the diorama were the sorts of people who belonged in Hatta, not me. Yet the model tent seemed to suggest that in a world that contained so many different cultures, the Arab culture of just a generation ago was the curiosity, not the Western culture of the present day guests. The diorama gave the foreigners what they wanted, I suppose—a safe taste of the exotic. And yet, what might have been perfectly all right in an ethnology museum in North America or Europe seemed out of place here, when something like the real thing was only an hour's drive away.

Nevertheless, there was a real history here, and as soon as we drove back off the hotel grounds, we were in that history again. We drove to the foot of the watchtower for one last look at Hatta. There was a visible history in the towers and the architecture of the houses, and there was an invisible history that remained in attitudes and values and customs. There was history and sociology "lite," the interpreted history that showed on the surface and which any foreigner could glean from guidebooks and replicas and restored villages before retreating to the comfort of the bar and the hotel room. There was the history of the imaginative and uninformed, who could see what they wanted to see. But there was also the real history, the flow of people and events that led from the past to the present, that had been interrupted and destroyed and rebuilt, and that kept on flowing and defining the character of the place. To find this history required more searching.

Here on the Arabian peninsula are ancient cities that traded with the Sumerians and Babylonians, that lined the route that brought incense to the Romans, and that traded with India and China long before Marco Polo made his way along the Silk Road to the court of Kubla Khan. Yet they seem just strange and unfamiliar names on a map to those who do not know this history. It is the search for this history that is the real exploration of the exotic.

PART TWO People

The ways we miss our lives are our lives.

—Randall Jarrell,
"The Girl in the Library"

Windows into the Emirates

Arriving in the Emirates had been easy, easier than any time I had ever come to a Middle Eastern country. Finding my way into the society was infinitely more difficult. When I had taught before in Egypt and Saudi Arabia, I had lived in apartment buildings inside the cities of Mansoura, Egypt, and Riyadh, Saudi Arabia. My neighbors were Arabs, and my friends were my Arab women colleagues. Here, I suddenly found myself living the sort of life that most Western expats lived in the Middle East. The university was about ten miles outside the city of Sharjah, and faculty lived on campus. In effect, I was living on a compound. Most of my neighbors were westerners, and when the fall semester began, I found most of my colleagues were Western men. The few Arab women professors taught in other departments. For the first time in almost twenty years, most of the people I knew were Western.

I had to find a way into the society if I were going to know where I was. I did have an Arab woman friend who lived in Dubai, a Palestinian who was married to an Emirati businessman. My students sometimes wrote and talked about their lives and their country, and the girls, particularly, liked to chat about themselves. They were hardly a cross-section of

Emirati society, however, because only very liberal parents would send their girls to a coeducational university like AUS. And finally, I had my memories of Laila, an Emirati girl I had known in the United States who had been more eager to find a way out of her society than I was now to find a way into it.

These were the doors that were open to me. They led into the private rooms of women who faced various kinds of closed doors themselves. Individual people's lives are shaped by the society that surrounds them, however, and the ways that people respond to their restrictions define who they are. The relationship between a person and society is like a line drawing. The blank spaces outside the figure are the invisible social conventions, and the lines themselves that define the figure are the ways in which a person has accepted or resisted her society's limits. By looking long enough at the various lines, one begins to see the shape of the blank spaces outside the lines.

For the first few weeks I tried to find my bearings within the compound. On the surface, the campus was beautiful, a garden in the desert. Seen from the air, it must have looked like an oasis, or a mirage, all those palatial buildings out where the white salt flats met the beginnings of the dunes. But it was a beauty I could appreciate only from indoors. Outside, the temperature was over 110 degrees, cooling down only into the low nineties at night, when I would walk out to take a moonlight swim in the faculty swimming pool. During the day, I walked only from my apartment to the air-conditioned bus that drove me the half-mile to work and then home again. The outside world could have been a mural painted on a window. The only people who were outside during the day were the Indian workmen, the gardeners who tended all those lovely flowering bushes and the construction workers who worked all day in the blazing heat putting up what would become air conditioned dormitories for students. Perhaps the outdoor world was real only to these workmen.

Whether I was on the inside looking out at the world, or on the outside of people trying to look into where we all were, I felt as if I were on the wrong side of a thick and discolored pane of glass. I began looking hard for ways to get through it.

Afaf

When Afaf, my Palestinian friend, came over in her four-wheel drive to take me away to spend the weekend at her home in Dubai, I was more than ready to go. Her big SUV pulled up in front of my apartment. Afaf, looking fit and vigorous, her short wiry brown hair wind blown, jumped out of the car and hugged me. She was in shorts and a T-shirt, but she looked different than she had in the United States. She had never been exactly pretty—her features were too large—but now radiating happy self-confidence, she had a vitality that went beyond prettiness.

Afaf lived on the edge of the desert in a development so new that the streets, still unnamed, were of sand and the four-wheel drive was really the only safe way to get in and out. There were a few other houses in the area, and about a half-mile away were a mosque and a little grocery store. From one window of her house, we had a view of the unspoiled desert, and from the other, a construction site. On the way in, she had pointed out a few tumbledown corrugated steel shacks. "This is where the workmen live," she told me, "except that now, when it's so hot, they usually sleep outside, under the equipment." The disparity between the beautiful new homes and the living conditions of the workmen obviously bothered her.

Inside, her home was spacious, modern, and tastefully furnished in beige and pale blue. Behind the house were a garden and swimming pool. As soon as we came in, Firdous, the maid, a pretty young Indian woman who padded around the house barefoot, started unpacking the groceries we had picked up on our way. Afaf spoke to her in Arabic. "Firdous doesn't know much English," she explained, "But she's picked up enough Arabic that we can talk to each other."

I wondered how one picked up Arabic. I'd been living off and on in the Middle East now for close to twenty years, and I had never met a language so resistant to being picked up.

Firdous brought us some cold sodas in the living room and Afaf started to tell me about her life here, which was very different from her life as a graduate student in the United States, when I had first known her. I had liked her then not just because she was a warm, intelligent woman, but because she had given me a sense of what America looked like from the perspective of an outsider who was not hoping to become an insider. She had tried hard to understand America but did not always like what she saw. She was ambivalent about America's wealth and power, particularly the latter, because it seemed to her to be used in the interests of wealthy Americans, at the expense of the world's poor. I also don't think she liked most Americans very much. To her, Americans seemed overly concerned with privacy and "personal space." (She hadn't understood at all why a pregnant stranger had been offended when she patted the woman's tummy and congratulated her, for instance.) She had measured America and Americans against her memories of home and her reading of the noble ideals that are part of a Western humanist education—but this didn't necessarily make her insights or criticisms wrong. And I liked her.

Now, she smiled more and seemed more confidant. Perhaps it was because in America she had been foreign and almost poor, whereas here she was wealthy and far less foreign. Our situations were now reversed. I was the foreigner who was out of her element, trying to understand, but a little uncomfortable with what was different.

At first, we just talked about the neighborhood. "Everyone is Emirati where we live," she began. "The westerners and the middle-class Indians live in the high rises downtown, and the Emiratis keep moving further and further out into the desert to get away from them. It's sort of like 'white flight' in the States, I suppose, except that they aren't really fleeing crime. It's just that they want to be among themselves." I thought of asking why, but I guessed the answer. It can make life less confusing, although considerably less interesting, to be among people who, one imagines, share one's view of the world. This wasn't the Dubai I had seen, but then, the Dubai I had seen was the very one that these Emiratis wanted to get away from. Did she want to get away from that world too?

"I'd like the world to be different. I'd like the rich not to be so rich and so self-absorbed. But I don't think we are likely to have a socialist revolution anytime soon," she said with a laugh.

Afaf and her husband Ahmad were not typical Emiratis, but they were not unusual among Arab intellectuals of their (and my) generation. They had been shaped by an era of secular political activism, and I suspected that era was now over. Their children lived in a very different world, a world with more money and less politics. In subtle and not-so-subtle ways, the money seemed to dissolve the edges of the sort of idealism that had defined their parents' lives, just as it had for the 1960s generation in America.

Once a bit of a radical, Afaf now lived in an expensive house and had a maid, while her four children went to one of the most exclusive private schools in the country and took lessons in horseback riding and sailing. The family seemed to have every material thing anyone wanted. And yet, what was Afaf to do? Deny her children the sort of things their friends had to spare them the corruption of wealth? I doubted if this would work.

The changes in values troubled Afaf. "The children don't like to go back to the West Bank with me," she told me. "They think Palestine is poor and dirty, and they think we must be very stupid to let our country get into such a state." She sighed. "When they are older, they'll learn more about politics and history, and then perhaps they will understand."

She was also ambivalent about the whole system of imported domestic workers, perhaps because she understood its history and causes. "As soon as people here started getting money," she told me, "they began moving out of the traditional extended families where the older parents and the grown sons and daughters-in-law all lived under one roof and shared the work. The money made it possible for a man to be the head of his own household while his father was still alive. But even though people started living in nuclear families, they kept up the traditions of the constant family visits and the guests and all of the things that went with a big household and were too much for one woman to manage alone. You can hire a maid from Indonesia or India and pay her less for a month than a middle-class Emirati woman would spend on a dress, so of course people started hiring maids. The maids are here to support their parents, or to save for a dowry for their daughters."

Later in the evening, when we had finished supper (cooked by Firdous under Afaf's direction, with me sitting on a chair watching), it was cool enough to sit outside by the pool. Over coffee, Afaf began to tell me the aspects of the housemaid system that bothered her the most. We had both written about this topic, and she knew that what troubled me was the lack of legal protection for these women. But what troubled Afaf was a more maternal concern. "Most of these maids are married women who have children that are being raised by somebody else so the woman can come here and make some money, and in a lot of cases, she ends up spending more time with the Emirati woman's children than their mother does. So many children here are being raised by series of maids, while their aunts or grandmothers back in their own country are raising the maids' children. All around the Indian Ocean, children are being raised without their mothers. It's an awful system."

"It's because a mother's love has no monetary value," I suggested.

"It has to do with status and social power too," she said thoughtfully, "and maybe independence. You may look at Firdous and see a poor, exploited woman, and that's partly true. But she's here because her husband back in India used to beat her, and this job gives her a way of living away from him and supporting herself. And now that she is making some money, her husband wants her to come back. Suddenly she's an asset, not a burden." Afaf sighed. "She'll probably go back to him again when her contract is up, and as soon as she's not making money, he'll probably beat her. But of course, she will be with her children again too."

"And there's no way she could bring her children with her?"

"No." She said simply. I had heard that a foreign worker had to make a certain amount in order to bring her family with her, and a maid just didn't make that much. The maids were contracted through a company that determined the wages. Even if Afaf had wanted to pay Firdous enough to bring her children with her, it would have been difficult. And where would the maid's children live? Afaf and Ahmad's house was large, but not big enough for two families.

We watched the moon come up over the horizon while the children splashed around in the water and Firdous washed the supper dishes inside. "I suppose I should say that this is a good system for me, because if we lived like people here did thirty years ago, I'd be living in my mother-in-law's house and she would be making the decisions about my children." In traditional Arab extended families, I knew, children were considered the responsibility of the household, not of their parents alone, and in fact, some families would consider a young mother to be too inexperienced to raise a child properly. "With a maid," she went on, "I'm able to live in my own house and work outside my home if I want to. And of course Firdous is doing the same work she would be doing at home, except that she's doing it in a nicer kitchen without anyone smacking her around."

"Sounds like you're saying it's not so bad after all," I suggested. I felt odd criticizing, sitting there enjoying a luxury I hadn't paid for, and yet what I had seen of the same system in

Saudi Arabia had outraged me. I knew instances of maids being beaten and even raped while the local government sided with the employers. I also felt that it wasn't particularly good for children to have a series of maids helping to raise them. I thought of my friend in Saudi Arabia, whose three-year-old daughter had been so upset when their maid went back to the Philippines that she'd cry whenever my friend left the room, convinced that her mother was about to leave forever, too. I thought of an American woman I'd known in Saudi Arabia who was shocked when she returned to the States and her ten-year old haughtily refused to help with the housework. "I'm not the maid," the little girl had announced. She wasn't just being a spoiled brat; the only person she had ever seen doing physical work was a person she had learned to regard as her inferior.

"I am not saying it isn't bad," Afaf said a little sharply. "I'm saying that it's not so bad for me. It's not good for Firdous's children, and I feel very guilty about this. But it's because of her that I am free to spend time with my own kids. I treat Firdous and all the maids I've had politely, and I try to be generous about money. That's all I can do."

"But not everybody is like you," I pressed.

"That's true," she said. "But it's not because people who have maids are awful. It's because the system is awful. It's because this is the only way two different levels of third-world women can get any control over their lives, and so they grasp at it whatever the risks." And of course, Afaf wasn't in a position to change the laws or the system so that maids could bring their children with them. This was the closed door in front of Afaf. If she did her own housework, few people would understand that it was because of her ideals about equality. They would just think she was too cheap to hire a maid. After all, in the Emirates, having a maid was so inexpensive that even the unemployed Emiratis who lived on government subsidies had maids. If she didn't have a maid, Afaf would have less time for her children and career, and her in-laws and neighbors would criticize her. Perhaps a well-connected Emirati woman could set an example, but not a foreigner.

I had the luxury of not having to think about these problems very much. What was a closed door for Afaf was a door that I could go in and out whenever I chose. I was a guest and a visitor in her world, and it was easy to just enjoy what it had to offer and then leave. Her home and its setting on the edge of the desert were beautiful, and the children were lively and friendly. I played with them, racing them across the swimming pool and playing computer games, all of which I invariably lost. And at night, we walked in the desert outside the house and looked at the moon and listened to the stillness.

"I love the desert," Afaf told me. "This isn't my country, but there is something about the desert that's in our blood." She pointed out a cluster of lights on the horizon and told me that it was Sharjah, only a five-minute drive across the desert, a half hour's drive by the road. "When I was working in Sharjah," she told me, "I used to come home at night across the desert road, and sometimes I'd stop the car and just look at stars and feel how quiet everything was."

Students

When my students began writing and I began discussing their papers with them and getting to know them, I had windows into other worlds. My women students did not live the way Afaf did, but they also didn't live like one another. The Emirati girls lived one life, and Arabs from the Levant another, and the girls from the other Gulf countries a different life still. Although the rules differed somewhat from one family to another, the traditional Emirati girls lived at home until they married, and when they were not in school they were usually with their families whenever they went out in public. These girls could go out shopping with their mothers, visit their girlfriends, and talk to male classmates at school, but they couldn't meet with boys outside of school, at least not if they wanted to preserve their reputations.

Shamsa was a very pretty girl from Dubai who wore the traditional *abayah* and *shillah* but allowed enough of her hair to show to frame her face. She came to see me because she had written a paper about friendship, in which she had talked about how a girl she thought was her good friend had betrayed her.

"How did she betray you?" I asked. "You have to give a specific example so your readers know what you mean," I explained.

She chewed her lip nervously. Finally she said, "She told people terrible things about me. All my respectable friends stopped talking to me. It was awful. I only thank God my parents didn't hear these things, even though they would know they weren't true." She hesitated and then blurted out, "She said I went to the beach and talked to boys." "Talked to" might have been a euphemism, but probably not exactly, because talking to boys in itself would be a breach of propriety. "If you talk to boys openly," an Egyptian girl had once told me, "everyone wonders what you must be doing when people aren't watching."

It was the action of her false friend that upset her, not the code of behavior she was expected to follow, and yet she did have a sense of something missing, something wrong. Her brother was studying in the United States, and she envied the independence this gave him. "He can do things for himself," she told me. "He knows how to rent an apartment and cook for himself. He can travel by himself. He knows how to talk to strange people. I don't know how to do any of those things. It makes me feel very stupid. One time our parents were out and it was the maid's day off, and he was laughing at me because I didn't even know how to cook an egg. He ended up making supper for us."

Of course, nothing about propriety prevented her from learning how to cook. But having a maid had kept her from ever needing to learn. Everything else—traveling, talking to strangers—she couldn't really do, not as an unmarried girl from a traditional family who hoped to get married. Only after she married could she do anything on her own. I have heard Western feminists declare that Arab women are treated like chattel. This really isn't true, and probably more accurately describes how Western men viewed Western women a few hundred years ago. But traditional Arab families do treat young women like children, at least until they are married. And of course the man a woman married would be someone selected by her family, not someone she had met on her own and fallen in love with. It was much the same among upper class girls in Europe and America a hundred years ago.

And as with the Victorians, the point of the restrictions seemed not to be just to keep young women virginal, but to keep them ignorant and dependent as well. A Palestinian girl commented on this in a paper. "For Syrian, Palestinian, and Lebanese ladies, it is very important to get an education. To Emirati families, the most important thing is for the girl to get married. I had an Emirati friend who was at the top of her class in high school, but her parents took her out of school because they were afraid that if she became too educated, no one they knew would want to marry her. I used to call her all the time and talk to her about school, but after a while, she asked me not to call anymore because it made her too sad."

Some of the Emirati girls whose families did approve of education took every advantage of it. These girls threw themselves into their work and used their good grades to prove to themselves that they could accomplish something worthwhile on their own. But Shamsa was not one of these girls. She stopped attending class regularly, and whenever I saw her on campus, she would be sitting with her girlfriends or talking into her mobile phone. Perhaps ignoring her schoolwork was a form of passive rebellion against parents who must, after all, have wanted her to be educated or they wouldn't have sent her to college. Giving up was easier, and perfectly respectable, and of course she didn't really need an education anyway, since she would never be required to earn her own living. The combination of wealth and powerlessness produced a corrosive compound that could eat away at self-respect and character, unless one had the self-knowledge and determination to fight against it. Only some of the young women had this kind of inner strength.

The difficulties of Emirati women (and perhaps of Emirati men as well) were increased by the fact that other girls in the Emirates were outwardly living much freer lives. These were the girls from poorer Arab countries whose families were working in the Emirates. These girls could play sports, go out with their girlfriends, and even go out in mixed groups. Although they weren't allowed to date, they could at least meet and talk to the sorts of men they might later marry. They came from countries with fewer restrictions on women to begin with, and the affluence and relative anonymity of Dubai gave them even more freedom, since aunts and grandfathers who might be upset by their conduct were back home. Of course, they still had the close family ties and the emphasis on premarital virginity that are part of Arab social ethics, and their families often decided things for them, such as where they would go to college and what they could major in. (Several girls and even a few boys were angry at finding themselves at the American University of Sharjah, when they had hoped to go to college in the United States.) Nevertheless, they were much freer than the Emirati girls.

Many of the non-Emirati girls had parents who felt that their daughters could grow up only by making their own decisions and facing the consequences. As long as those decisions didn't involved sexual behavior, they could even make stupid decisions and learn from them. Luma, a Palestinian girl who lived in Dubai, wrote about the time she decided to go bungee jumping, her point being how stupid it is to succumb to peer pressure and do something you don't want to do for fear your friends will think you're afraid.

"My friends' mothers wouldn't let them try," she wrote, "but my Mom said to go ahead if I really wanted to, so I didn't have any excuse. I didn't want to do it, but my friends all started teasing me and making clucking noises, so I did it. It was awful. There I was hanging upside down bouncing above the ocean being scared out of my wits, and all I could think about was what an idiot I had been to put myself through something like that just so people wouldn't laugh at me."

I could no more imagine Shamsa bungee jumping, or writing an original and intelligent paper about learning from mistakes, than I could imagine her turning into a giraffe. It was as if the Emirates contained parallel universes, each governed by its own set of physical laws but visible to one another.

Added to these two universes was that of Western women, whose lives Emiratis saw, or thought they saw, on their TV screens and whom they saw in real life at a distance in stores. I imagine this life seemed both glamorous and dangerous, and I'm also sure that only people who had read a great deal or who had lived in the West knew how different this image was from the way Western women really lived. It couldn't have been easy to deal with. I asked Afaf about this, when her boys were watching their favorite Spice Girls video for the third time that weekend. How does a boy who has grown up with that image marry a sheltered, conventional girl whom he hardly knows?

"Ginger Spice is the fantasy; the girl in the *abayah* is the reality," Afaf said quickly. "They know that."

I wasn't so sure. It seemed to me that the closed room in which so many Emirati women (and men) lived contained a window into a virtual reality that they had no way of knowing wasn't real.

Laila

Laila was one of the few people I had ever known who had decided to find out for herself what was beyond that door. I first heard of her back in Washington when my husband mentioned that one of his graduate students had a problem. The grad student had taught for a semester at a university in the Emirates, and suddenly one of her former students, Laila, had shown up on her doorstep. Laila was almost twenty-one years old, with about a thousand dollars in her purse but no degrees or skills with which to earn more when that ran out. She had sold her gold jewelry (most upper class Arab girls have a very good supply), bought herself a ticket to the United States, convinced the officials at the American embassy to give her a five-year tourist visa, and arrived in the States planning to start a new life. She didn't know that she couldn't get a job without a green card, and she didn't know that she would need her high school diploma and her college records to get into a university in the United States. She could speak English, but she couldn't read or write it very well. All she knew was that she didn't want to go back.

At the time, I couldn't really understand what had made her run away, or be so determined to stay. I had taught for years in Saudi Arabia, where girls were far more restricted than in the Emirates, and they didn't try to run away, even women who were much older and who had lived in the West. Family ties and the sense of identity and security that these ties gave were always more important to them than personal freedom. I wondered what it was it about Laila, and the Emirates, that made her do what she did and gave her the strength to live with the consequences of her decision.

When I first met Laila, everyone I knew seemed to regard her more as a problem than as a person. The graduate student found her a burden. She had allowed Laila to stay with her for two weeks, but she didn't have either the space or the money to let her stay longer. From there, Laila had gone to stay with a series of Arab American families, mostly Egyptian friends of my husband. These families were willing to let her live with them temporarily but saw her as a very wild girl who might be redeemed if she were treated strictly enough. Even Afaf was a bit dubious about her, fearing that Laila simply wasn't mature enough to realize that all lives had problems and limits, and that she had run to America thinking she would live the life she had seen in the movies. Americans who heard her story expressed great admiration for her courage, but none of them offered her a place to live. In a way, I guess, she was a symbol to both groups. To the Arab Americans, she was one of them, but one who had strayed. They complained about the way she dressed (shorts, tight jeans, and tank tops, just like many of the non-Gulf Arab girls at the college) and about the fact that she didn't know how to cook or do housework. They were convinced that she had run away in order to have sex and would become a prostitute if they didn't intervene. She had, after all, rejected the conventions that they had accepted, and she was a threat. To the Americans, she had done a laudable thing, but she was not one of them and her plight finally did not concern them. A few talked about trying to find an asylum lawyer for her, but no one was willing to pay the fees. I let her stay with me for a few weeks, but I lived in a very small apartment and I didn't have room for her either.

I liked Laila. She was a mature young woman, pretty, polite, and lively, but not in any wild or reckless way. While she stayed with me, we chatted and took walks together, and I taught her how to swim, which she was very eager to learn.

"I never got a chance to do this at home," she explained. "So many things I never got a chance to do." She never got a chance to learn any sports, or dance, or even take a walk by herself.

While we walked along the bike paths in Washington's parks and trails, she told me about her life. She lived with her father, who had divorced her mother and lived with his new wife and their children, all much younger than Laila. Her stepmother wasn't unkind to Laila, but she wasn't warm either. Nor was her own mother, who was also remarried and had children by her new husband. To both parents, I gathered, she was a somewhat painful reminder of a marriage that hadn't worked. Her parents did their duty by her, but she wasn't emotionally close to either of them. It wasn't exactly a lack of love, but it was a love without intimacy. Yet they had obviously given her more than she acknowledged, or she wouldn't have been so balanced and self-confident in the middle of such criticism and uncertainty.

She finally solved her problem herself. Acting against the advice of all her benefactors, who told her that if the Emirati government found out about her they would surely seize her and send her back to her family, she went to the Emirati embassy and asked for their help. In fact, the embassy response was extremely compassionate. They told her that they could give her a clerical job there at the embassy, if her father agreed, and after some persuasion, he did. Without a green card, the only place she could legally work was at an embassy, and fortunately the embassy was willing to overlook her lack of skills and to train her. Laila was able to stop being a mobile houseguest and moved into a small apartment that she shared with a graduate student, this time able to pay her share of the rent. She got her college transcripts and started attending university part time, again courtesy of the Emirati embassy.

"So I didn't end up a drug addict or a prostitute, like those Arab ladies thought I would. I'm all right," she told me when I went to visit her in her apartment. In fact, she seemed more than all right, I thought, as she excitedly showed me pictures of a trip to New York she had taken with a group of her girlfriends, mostly young Latin American women who worked at various embassies. It had been easy for her to make friends with them, she said, because they had thought she was a Latina when they first met her. She had also learned to drive and had just bought a car, also a source of great excitement for her. And she was taking jazz dancing lessons. "Is this the kind of life you hoped for when you ran away?" I asked her.

She shrugged. "It's not as exciting as I thought. I don't have a boyfriend. I have to work harder than I expected. But I don't really mind not having a boyfriend and having to work hard. I've learned how to do things for myself, and this is what I wanted."

Now, in the Emirates myself, I was able to understand more about why Laila had run away and what had given her the courage to leave. She hadn't left because she wanted either sexual or political freedom. She left because she didn't want to be treated like a child when, in fact, she was an adult. She wanted to control what she did with her own body, not necessarily sexually, but in sports and dance and travel and dress, and not to be immobilized by conventions while other girls she knew (the non-Gulf Arabs) seemed to be able to do as they pleased. If she hadn't seen other girls acting differently, hadn't been able to try on the Western costume, she wouldn't have wanted to leave. If she had real intimacy with her family, it might not have been worth trading for autonomy. Many other Arab girls were willing to give up real independence for love and closeness, or even for security, and the trade was not necessarily a bad one. But the windows of Laila's society had let her see that it might be possible for her to gain control over the direction of her life, and so she had left her own world for the world outside that window. Something inside her had given her the courage to risk everything.

She also left because the door in front of her was closed but not locked. Literally, she could run away because she had the money to do so and because there was no law saying she couldn't leave the country without a male relative, as is the case in Saudi Arabia, for instance. But in a larger sense, the door was unlocked because the Emiratis involved were compassionate people. Her father was willing to give his consent for her to work and to give her money to repay her Arab American hostesses because he cared more about her than he did about the scandal she had created by leaving home. Other fathers, from other Arab countries, could literally have killed their daughters for doing what she did, knowing that the law would look the other way if family honor were involved. The embassy officials could have told her there was nothing they could do for her, since they certainly weren't under any obligation to help her out. Instead, they did everything they legally could for her. She had broken all their conventions concerning acceptable behavior for a young woman, and I'm sure that all of the men at the embassy would have been appalled if their daughters had acted as she did. Yet they had not seen her as a symbol of transgression, but as a woman from their country in need of their help. This is more revealing about Emirati society, I think, than the fact the Laila wanted to run away from it.

From these glimpses into Emirati society, I created patterns, even though I knew that my knowledge was very limited, and that the same things could be shaped into entirely different patterns. I created these patterns because I wanted to understand what I had seen and was discontent with random impressions.

The patterns were in me as much as in what I saw. American society has its own limits and boundaries, its own conventions and assumptions, its own kinds of unhappiness. Different boundaries shaped me. I had my own fears and responded to different assumptions that I didn't necessarily accept but found difficult to ignore. From within the boundaries of a self shaped by American society, I could look into the windows of lives different from my own, seeing patterns of existing that were defined by the social spaces of another place, and discover the doors into this society.

Students

Teaching and Learning Across Cultures

I had a glimpse of the shameless, marvelous, shattering absurdity with which the plots of real life, though not of fiction, are improvised.

—Alice Munro

During my first few months in the Emirates, as I tried to understand the society around me, I also faced a more immediate and pressing task. I had to try to understand my students and learn how to teach them. What I learned from teaching them, however, gave me many more insights into contemporary Middle Eastern society than I would have gathered if I had just read and observed and talked to Emirati intellectuals my own age. I learned, for one thing, about my students' attitudes toward the roles of men and women and about their feelings concerning the relative merits of Western society and their own. These attitudes were often paradoxically both more traditionally Middle Eastern and more flexible than I had assumed. I also gained some insights into the complex relationship between contemporary Middle Eastern society and Western pop culture.

The students were different from the international students I had previously taught. They were a strange mixture of cultures, backgrounds, and attitudes. In fact, because some of them were from mixed marriages and many of them had visited or lived in other countries, different cultures often blended within the same student. Some were Emirati, but more were Palestinian, Syrian, Iranian, Indian, or Lebanese. Some of the students were Christians, especially the Indians and Palestinians, and a few of the Indians were Hindus; but most of the students were Muslim. Unlike most of the students I had taught in the past, they were all either freshmen or sophomores, as the university was only in its second year. Some of the students were only sixteen or seventeen, while others were in their mid-twenties, having attended and dropped out of other universities before coming to AUS. What they had in common, however, was that they seemed to have been raised on a steady diet of American popular culture without having any other kind of contact with American society, except perhaps a shopping trip to New York. They had also lived most of their lives in traditional societies, and many of them were in a classroom with the opposite sex for the first time in their lives. All of these things made them both interesting and annoying to teach.

For one thing, many of them were rather childish. They were all bright enough to have learned how to speak a second language fairly well, and almost all of them were very polite when I talked to them individually. However, many of them came to class late, handed in assignments late, and talked to one another during class. When they got poor marks, they argued and complained at length—politely, but energetically. They weren't stupid or hostile, just immature. Scolding them was like spanking cats. They just looked at me as if I were suffering from a bout of temporary insanity, waited for me to get over it, and continued as usual. Agreeing that this was a problem, some of the Arab teachers told me that the students had picked up these attitudes from watching American television. "They've all watched *Saved by the Bell* and think this is how American students act in class," a Moroccan colleague told me. Apparently, acting like an American, or the way they thought Americans acted, was very cool. And yet, perhaps in some ways, contact with American popular culture also made some of them more open to more complex versions of Western thinking about Western societies.

And so, somewhat to my surprise, learning actually did take place. I learned about who they really were underneath some of their pseudo-American poses, and they learned, among other things, that there was more to Western thinking than a lifetime of television viewing had led them to believe. I found that they were interested in talking about the moral and social issues in the literature they were reading and in giving their opinions, especially when we discussed works that concerned the position of women in society. I think this was because these works seemed to them to reflect the real world they lived in, not the world of Western television, and raised larger questions about the nature and structure of human societies.

The position of women in Middle Eastern societies is changing, as men and women both reassess traditional attitudes. In fact, even many fairly traditional people were questioning women's roles in society. Islam did give women important rights, many Muslim feminists have argued, but male authorities had misinterpreted Islam to deny women these rights because women had been too uneducated to know what their rights were. In fact, this re-evaluation has been going on since the beginning of the twentieth century, but now, ideas that were once the domain of the Westernized upper classes in colonial countries have become the subjects of debate among more ordinary people throughout the Middle East. This is why the work we studied led us into larger discussions. And of course, the classroom was one of the few places where young men and women could have a serious group discussion about gender roles and expectations.

The two pieces that concerned my students most were works that probably wouldn't elicit much excitement from American students today: Alice Munro's touching and humorous short story, "An Ounce of Cure," and more surprisingly, Henrick Ibsen's *A Doll's House,* which to them was shocking and enlightening. How they responded to these works helped me to understand them better, as well as the social forces that had shaped them.

"An Ounce of Cure" is a deceptively simple story about a young girl, probably about fourteen or fifteen, in a small town in Canada in the 1950s. She has a crush on a boy who pays her a great deal of attention and then drops her. She suffers not only the pains of unrequited love, but the painful delight of making herself the heroine of a melodrama, with her friends admiring her suffering and themselves for being so loyal and supportive. Unfortunately, one night while she is babysitting in the home of a family that, unlike her own, drinks alcohol, she notices the liquor bottles sitting on the counter and decides that a drink would balm her broken heart. Since she hasn't seen people preparing drinks, she assumes that a person just pours whiskey into a water glass and tosses it down like soda. She also assumes that the effect will be immediate, so that when she doesn't feel anything but a burning throat after downing a six ounce glass of whiskey, she has another one.

The result is that the floor hits her in the face fifteen minutes later and she barely makes it to the bathroom before vomiting. Terrified at what is happening to her, she calls her girlfriends to help her out, and these friends bring a couple of boys with them, who proceed to play records and turn the whole evening into a party. The next time she feels like vomiting, she doesn't make it to the bathroom, and her girlfriends remove her vomit-stained skirt and blouse to wash them, while the girl wraps herself up in an afghan and waits for her clothes to dry. At this point, the family returns home to find their babysitter in her slip (and an afghan) and a group of boys and girls dancing to their records.

To make matters worse, the girl's mother tries to mend the problem by explaining to the couple that the girl is a bit immature and unstable, and suggests that her crush on the boy who dropped her is the source of her strange behavior. Word of both versions becomes public, and the town and school are divided between those who think she is a slut and those who think she's crazy. The girl is a social outcast for the next year, until someone else does something worse and people forget about her own escapade.

What interests the girl most about the whole episode, however, is that she not only gets over her crush, but she becomes fascinated by watching the way the whole drama unfolds and by the mistakes in judgment of the supposedly more knowing adults. She starts looking at the outside world and understanding other people's motives rather than focusing on her own feelings. She grows up. As the story ends, she is looking back on the events as an adult woman. At the funeral of a relative, she returns to her hometown and accidentally meets the object of her former crush, now a grown man. He gives her a smirk of recognition; she smiles politely and pretends she doesn't know him.

One would think that students acquainted with American television would have understood the story fairly easily, but this was not the case, and the ways they misunderstood it and the issues they raised were very enlightening. First, it was interesting to me that almost all the students ignored the relatively happy ending and instead focused on the causes of the girl's becoming a local scandal. In fact, they tended to focus particularly on the ways in which North American society differed from their own, and saw these differences as the source of what they at first viewed as a horrifying event. (American expats, I've noticed, do the same thing in reverse when anything inconvenient happens to them in the Middle East. If those people were just more like us, the thinking goes, they wouldn't have this problem.) Therefore, when we began to discuss the story, many of the students wanted to see it as cautionary tale about the evils of drink, since most of them were Muslims and had been taught that drinking alcohol was sinful. Drink was the cause of the narrator's downfall.

And many of them, especially the boys, blamed the girl for her actions, declaring that only a very wild and unbalanced girl would drink, or have a crush on a boy, for that matter, since she was far too young to marry.

They were also horrified by her having been "half naked" in a room with boys, as though she had deliberately set out to do this. Essentially, they accepted at face value the rumors the town repeated, just as if they hadn't read what actually happened. To many of them, the appearance of sexual "misconduct" was as bad as if she had indeed gotten drunk at a party and done a striptease in front of the boys. I think perhaps they felt this way because many Arab societies (or those I am familiar with, at least) do place a considerable emphasis on the appearance of propriety, and it was hard for them to see that propriety and morality might be different. I also noted with interest that those students who adopted American clothing styles and body language were among the most adamant in condemning the "decadence" of Western society, or what they thought was Western society.

I was amazed, however, at the number of both men and women students who were willing to modify their views, perhaps because their exposure to popular culture had taught them that other views existed. They knew that Western teenagers sometimes got drunk, went to parties, and had sex. What they didn't know was that some people in Western society would find this scandalous. They thought all Western teenagers got drunk and had sex, and indeed that orgies were a basic feature of Western society. More important, it never seemed to occur to any of them that Western thinkers might criticize the smugness and hypocrisy of this "respectable" condemnation without condoning drunkenness and promiscuous sex. The brighter students found this more complex version of Western attitudes very interesting, once they understood it, but getting there took time.

I had to remind them that a slip covered as much of the girl's body as a dress would have, that a blanket covered her anyway, and that she was in a state of undress because her girlfriends had taken her clothes to wash them, not because she had felt an urge to undress in public. And besides, she had been too sick and befuddled to object. I also explained that in the girl's society, drinking was generally tolerated as long as it was done in moderation, by adults, although some people, such as the girl's family, would consider any drinking a moral weakness. I pointed out the fact that the girl had seen the couple she worked for having a drink with friends before they left, with no ill effects, and that the couple's outrage at finding their babysitter drunk was to a certain degree hypocritical. The girl was just doing what she had seen adults doing a few hours earlier, and the couple might well have been irresponsible in leaving liquor bottles out on the counter when there were children in the house (and the narrator was, after all, still a child). At this, I noticed several of the girls smiling and nodding.

And, I was interested to note, several of the girls explained in their journals (although not in class, in front of the boys) that early adolescence was a time of increased hormone production and that it was totally normal for a girl to have "romantic" feelings about a boy. Many of the girls also thought that the narrator was in fact a rather sympathetic character who was very much the victim of circumstances. She was made a scapegoat when both the other teenagers and the adults around her had done equally foolish things, one girl suggested. Bravely, she said this in class, while many of the boys looked disconcerted and others whispered to each other. I think what was happening, at least in the mind of that girl, was that "Western" behavior that before had seemed incomprehensibly bizarre (if entertaining) suddenly became familiar human behavior.

Having absolved the girl from serious blame (she was guilty of immaturity and poor judgment, I pointed out, but who in the world is mature at fifteen?), they then focused on the society and the adults as the culprits, which is to some degree what Munro is suggesting as well. But even after this shift in focus, they still concentrated at first on the ways in which Western and Middle Eastern society differed. Many of the students, especially the women, thought that the girl's mother should have been much more understanding about her crush and that they should have had heart-to-heart talks about the meaning of love. Then the girl wouldn't have felt so bad that she was tempted to drink, they reasoned. I think they measured the mother against the ideal Arab mother and found her lacking, as any realistically depicted woman would be when compared to an ideal. I suggested that a writer's purpose should not be to show the ideal, but rather to indicate the varieties of human behavior. We all know how an ideal mother would behave, I told them. What we might not know are some of the ways a good but somewhat confused person might behave. The mother is a well-meaning but rather insensitive woman, and her daughter obviously accepts this, especially after she is grown. Not all of the students bought this interpretation. But then, why should they? The point was that we were talking about it, and some of them were beginning to get the idea that literature was more than just the clever plots of movies.

And this discussion led to another, much more thought provoking one. Wasn't the problem, one boy suggested, that Canadian society had so many conflicting values? Some people tolerated drinking; some people condemned it. Teenage boys and girls were allowed to mix socially without adult supervision, and yet they were expected to behave with the same maturity and propriety as if adults were present and were pilloried when they did not. Wasn't this going to be awfully confusing to any child? Arab society was better in this case, he suggested, because everyone agreed that drinking was wrong. Even people who drank did so privately, and they didn't advocate it. And boys and girls didn't mix unsupervised in even the most liberal Arab societies until they were of marriageable age. Wasn't one of the problems with Western society in general that no one could agree on what was right or wrong? I thought he had a very shrewd point, and it seemed to me that Munro was indeed suggesting that in many ways conventional North American society of that time did expect too much maturity from children.

But whether uniformity of values was ultimately preferable to pluralism seemed to me much more debatable. Wasn't there also a considerable degree of pluralism within their own societies? They thought not, but that may have been because they were too young to have been exposed to values different from those of their families and the sorts of friends their families approved of. I also asked them what happened to the person who found he disagreed with his society's conventions. The Arab way, they told me, was usually to disagree privately while conforming publicly. We discussed whether this conformity was good for society, which is, after all, an unanswerable question. What surprised me was that they were more open to such discussions than most other Arab students I had taught, except for my graduate students in Egypt and Saudi Arabia, who were much more familiar with Western high culture than these students. Perhaps pop culture was a kind of foot in the door that made them open to more sophisticated thinking. In itself, pop culture seemed to be simply confusing, or to convince them that their own society and values were certainly better than the absence of values and social constraints they saw on American television. Coupled with literature, however, it could produce the beginnings of a real cosmopolitanism.

More ideas about the nature of society, relationships between men and women, convention, and the individual came out in their written work. To help them understand the ways in which plot, setting, and tone combine to convey theme, I had asked the students to select a story and explain how the idea of a story would change if the setting and tone were changed. Several of them decided to write about how "An Ounce of Cure" would be different in an Arab setting. They immediately found that the plot would have to change. Setting and plot are connected in a way that they hadn't thought about before, as I had hoped they would discover. Since Islam forbids alcohol (although alcohol is legal in many Islamic countries) they found it unlikely that the neighbors would have drunk in front of the girl, or left liquor bottles sitting around. She would have had to search for them, which in turn would have changed the girl's character. If the character were changed to be more aggressive and rebellious, the tone would less sympathetic and the theme would be murkier. Or the plot would have to be rewritten so the girl got stomach flu and instead of getting drunk, in which case the response of the neighbors would have seemed far crueler, which again would have changed their characters and the theme of the story. What all of the students consistently suggested, however, was that the ending would not have been as fortunate in an Arab setting. A girl who had been found half-clothed with a group of boys would suffer lasting disgrace.

"In Damascus today, if it became known that a girl had

done such a thing, the scandal would never die down," a Syrian boy told me. "People would remember, even after they stopped talking about it, and no reputable man would marry her. If she did marry, it would probably be to the sort of man who would throw it up to her every time she disagreed with him. That would be part of the reason he would marry such a girl."

"Even if she hadn't done anything sexual?" I asked.

"Oh, yes," he explained. "If she had actually done anything, her parents would have disowned her."

And how would the changes in plot and setting have affected the story's theme? Answering this question was beyond the abilities of most of the students, but one girl named Maha suggested that in the face of such disgrace and humiliation, the narrator would probably not have learned to focus her attention outward in such a constructive way.

"I think she would have focused on criticizing other people to make herself feel better. I think she would try to appear very proper and conventional, but she would be very bitter. In an Arab society, she would have had a far more difficult time."

This certainly explained why the students had ignored the upbeat ending. How can one see something as an embarrassing incident when in one's own society it would be a life-altering crisis? It was like transporting Hester Prynne and her Salem persecutors to a large American city in the 1990s and wonder-ing why they should think adultery and an illegitimate child were such a big deal.

Perhaps because this sad ending was so uncomfortable, Maha then had another idea. "I think, though, that the plot would be different in an Arab setting," she explained. "I think most Arab girls would have known better than to bring boys with them. If the neighbors just found a group of girls drunk and playing music, they would have been very angry and the girls would have been in big trouble, but it wouldn't have been a lasting scandal. Then the story could have ended just as Alice Munro had it end."

This level of thought delighted me. She wasn't saying that one society was better than the other. She was looking at the ways in which different societies structured human relationships, how this affected individual people's values and attitudes, and how fiction could reflect all of these things. Several of the girls asked to borrow my collection of Alice Munro's short stories so they could read more of her work.

I found their interest in discussing the nature of societies to be even stronger when we began to discuss Henrik Ibsen's *A Doll's House*. To westerners, the play can seem both so melodramatic and such a didactically feminist text that much modern criticism has centered on showing that Nora is not intended to be the flawless heroine. My American students have found Nora's behavior in the opening scenes so childish that they have asked me if she is supposed to be mentally retarded. But to my students at AUS in 1998, the play was as shocking as it was when it first appeared on the stage in Norway more than one hundred years earlier, if not more so.

Unlike Ibsen's first audience, however, many of the AUS students felt that Torvald was overbearing and condescending to Nora, and some boys expressed their disgust. "We have this sort of man in my country and I do not like them. They must be in charge and control everything in the household," one Lebanese boy wrote. But they were not expecting Nora to leave at the end. They sympathized with Nora but expected her to put her feelings toward Torvald aside and stay with him for the sake of the children.

The ending surprised the students, they told me, because this was not the way stories ended. I think perhaps they were expecting the conventional Hollywood happy ending, or at least they were expecting an ending that showed how things should be, rather than how they sometimes are. They were used to movies and TV programs that gave pat solutions to complex problems, after all, not works of literature that raised questions. Was Ibsen suggesting that Nora's leaving Torvald was a good thing? When the door slams, does Ibsen want us to cry or cheer? The usual reading, and the one that caused Shaw to find the play "as dull as ditch water," is that we are supposed to cheer. But I wasn't as sure myself, especially after reading some of the contemporary criticism. My students wanted an answer. Since I found the tone toward Nora and her decision a very debatable point, I started asking them questions that I thought would make the debate more meaningful.

Why, I asked them, did they suppose that Ibsen had not made Torvald a cruel bully, if he wanted us to approve of Nora's leaving him? In the scene in which he denounces her, he could have hit her as well. And why have him apologize, and even recognize the truth of some of her arguments? Why not just have him insist that she is a stupid woman without any sense of morality, as he does at first?

"Because that would just say that some men are really bad," one girl suggested. "It wouldn't say that his ideas are bad. Ibsen wants us to see that the problem is with his ideas, the way he values his reputation more than his wife, the way he treats her like a child."

And again we were into to the distinction between morality and socially acceptable behavior, and between legality and ethics. In the eyes of his society, I pointed out, Torvald has done nothing wrong. Nora has, in forging her father's signature, even though she did it to spare a dying man distress. Why didn't Ibsen create a character that was socially blameless, like the heroines of the nineteenth-century melodramas his audience was used to?

"Because he wanted us to think about it, and realize that society misjudges people?" a boy asked.

Good points, all. Then someone suggested that Nora was shallow and selfish as well. "She's just like a teenager," said one boy who was still a teenager himself. "If everything isn't perfect, she thinks it's worthless. Life isn't fair so she is going to kill herself. Her husband isn't the great hero she thought he was so she leaves him and her kids. If she were more grown up, she would stay and try to work out a better marriage. She'd realize that a person has to make the best of things that aren't perfect."

I thought this was a very intelligent insight. Nora probably isn't fully mature because she hasn't had the opportunity to mature. In this way, she was probably like some Arab women I had observed. Powerlessness in itself can be infantilizing, unless the woman is aware of the danger and struggles against it. And this interpretation certainly makes the play far more complex and thought provoking than if we see Nora as a feminist exemplar.

As we discussed the play, it became clear that these students viewed the play as a tragedy in ways that American students usually did not. The tragedy was a broken marriage and children being raised without a mother. Following that line of thought, Torvald isn't a villain, and Nora isn't a heroine, but a good person who is flawed by the same kind of rigid thinking that makes Torvald so judgmental and unsympathetic. It certainly makes sense that Nora would adopt some of Torvald's faults, since she has been shaped so much by his thinking. Moreover, even if Nora is somewhat confused and unhappy, she could still be a good mother to her children, probably better than the kindly but aging nanny could. (How many of my students, I wondered, had been raised by a series of nannies themselves?) After all, if motherhood really required total maturity and a happy marriage, I suspect the world would be seriously underpopulated. Thus in some ways, her decision is immature.

Then I brought up another point. Nora's problem is also that the rules have been changed. She carried out her role of the loving and self-sacrificing wife and mother, but Torvald failed to play his complementary role as her protector. And there is no law that will punish him for failing in this role. Many of the students agreed, although some still placed the blame primarily on Nora for the breakup of the marriage.

"It's the woman's responsibility to keep the family together," one boy asserted.

"I agree," a young woman said. "That's why God made women more compassionate and forgiving than men. So they could endure men's childishness as well as that of their children."

I then told them about Ibsen's alternative "happy ending," where Torvald forces Nora to look for a last time at their children, and she cries and decides to stay for their sakes.

Would that ending be more satisfying? I asked them. No, they thought. That made it seem that Nora was in the wrong completely and Torvald really was more mature.

"But wasn't that what you were just saying?" I asked them.

No, they said. What they wanted was some assurance that, although she was leaving, she would be back. They wanted another act, in which she did return. (That, I thought, would turn *A Doll's House* into *Kramer vs. Kramer.*) I suggested to them that if that had been the case, we wouldn't have had as much to think and talk about. Instead, we would have had a comfortable ending in which decent people always acted for the best, when life often revealed this not to be the case.

But they also found Nora's reaction shocking for a more complex reason. In their society, motherhood defined a woman. It wasn't just a rewarding responsibility and a part of who she was for a part of her life. A woman's children were an extension of herself that continued not only throughout her life but after her death. "They come out of her body and they are always part of her heart. They are the part of her that will live when she is dead," one young woman said. How, then, could any woman leave her children?

"Our Prophet teaches that your duty is first to your mother and second to your mother and third to your mother and then to your father," one girl quoted. And when one was an adult, one's duty to the mother also superseded duty to one's spouse. Nora's leaving her children struck my students as being almost as rash and hysterical as her earlier plan to kill herself to vindicate Torvald. I don't think that the nineteenth-century Europeans for whom the play was written felt this as strongly as my students did, or indeed that this idea of motherhood as permanent identity has been part of European and North American culture the way it is in Middle Eastern cultures.

What I realized from this discussion was that parts of Middle Eastern culture that seem at first to be the same as old-fashioned Western values are really not the same, because they come out of a different history and philosophy. The parallels were not exact and were often cultural false cognates.

What I also found in this discussion was a maturity and complexity of thought that is rare in any classroom. Perhaps it came from the degree to which these students were bicultural, from the fact that they were aware that other people held other values. Because they had been exposed to the existence of other values, they could begin to question some of their own values and to find what they truly believed.

Mohammad al-Murr's Map of Dubai

The only way to ever learn your way around here is to get really lost.

—American expat living in the UAE

Several years ago, the editor of a scholarly journal asked me to review two collections of short stories by an Emirati writer named Mohammad al-Murr. I suppose the editor thought that since I had reviewed Arabic novels before and had lived in Egypt and Saudi Arabia, it would be simple for me to understand and evaluate al-Murr's work. It was not. Reading a story without knowing the society that shaped it is like looking at a map of a city you have never seen.

After I had lived in the Emirates for a year, I began to understand the stories more fully because I began to get the help I needed to understand their social and literary context. The stories in turn helped me to understand the society around me. Reading the stories back in Washington, I could make no more sense of them than the map of Sharjah and Dubai that the university had so thoughtfully sent me. I assumed that when I was actually in the Emirates, however, I could compare the maps to the streets and the stories to my observations and begin to find my way around both. The stories were both the map and the territory, I figured, and each would help me understand the other so that I would come to know where I was culturally, just as the literal map and territory would help me understand where I was geographically.

This was true, but only to a degree. When I started driving around Sharjah and Dubai, I quickly learned that maps are not as useful as they might seem. For one thing, the streets were labeled on the map, but in the real world there weren't any street signs. The roundabouts all had signs, but these roundabouts were not labeled on the map. Worse, a wrong turn on a traffic circle could land me half way to Abu Dhabi, when my original destination had been the grocery store in Sharjah. I could easily do the same thing with the stories, I feared, if I didn't stop and ask somebody local what this map really meant.

Yet I never questioned whether trying to find my way around these stories was useful, even if I did end up in Abu Dhabi by mistake. I still think this is true. Short stories are often maps of inner spaces. They show what a writer sees beneath the surface of his society. There is no Winesburg, Ohio, on any map of the United States. Someone walking down the street in a small midwestern town in 1920 would probably have seen only the surface of pleasant neighborliness, not the obsession and loneliness and intensity that deformed and enriched the lives of Sherwood Anderson's characters. And yet, the surface that most people can agree upon is not necessarily what lasts. By the time I was growing up, the surface of small town America looked quite different than it did in Anderson's time. Yet, when I first read *Winesburg, Ohio*, I recognized where I lived. There is something there about America that has stayed true. There is a direct line between *Winesburg, Ohio* and Raymond Carver's *Where I'm Calling From,* because Carver's characters are calling from the same immense loneliness at the heart of America that the citizens of Winesburg tried so desperately to escape seventy years earlier.

Al-Murr's stories do the same thing, I think, except that there is a literal Dubai as well as a fictive one, and the preoccupations of his characters are different from those that haunt the characters in American short stories. The inner spaces stay the same in al-Murr's work, although the stories span about forty years, from the time when Dubai was a walled city that closed its gates at night to the time when men cruise the streets in expensive cars until the small hours. Al-Murr's characters often lead double lives and do everything to distract themselves from thinking about the meaning of the disjunction between their outward propriety and their secret dissipations, and between their public faces and their inner feelings. And yet, in al-Murr's hands, they become no less sympathetic to an American reader like me than Anderson and Carver's lonely and confused Americans.

In the stories that I found most accessible, these inner conflicts became as brittle and transparent as glass, although the stories themselves were still not exactly like short stories written in English. A Western reader filters out what is opaque, what she doesn't understand, and focuses on what is clear, even though it might not be the emphasis of the original stories. In these conflicts, what I see again and again are people who live conventional and outwardly respectable lives but have secret fantasies of romance and excitement, which they attempt to realize, sometimes to their regret.

In one story, "The Pleasure of the Night," Jasim, a married

man whose pregnant wife is waiting for him at home, decides to act out his fantasy of what his life would be if he were a carefree bachelor by driving around the streets at night looking for girls. Somewhat to his surprise, he finds one—not a foreign prostitute but a local girl in an *abayah* and *shillah* who readily gets into his car and agrees to go back to his friend's empty apartment with him. He assumes that the girl is acting out her own fantasy of escape and looking for sex and excitement, just as he is. Probably, he thinks, they will have a sexual encounter, but at any rate, he will have had an adventure. But if the girl is acting out a fantasy of her own, it certainly doesn't correspond with his. As soon as he gets her back to the apartment, she calls him her husband and insists on making dinner for him. Since there is little food in the flat, she wants to go to the neighbors to borrow the ingredients, which is of course the last thing he wants. The neighbors will be scandalized, and it will get back to his family. His reputation will be ruined. To keep the girl quiet, he suggests that they go out to eat instead, out to a cheap take-out place where nobody could possibly recognize him. But the girl still embarrasses him with loud, bizarre remarks—such as declaring that carrots are poisonous—either because she is crazy, as he thinks, or because she is acting out her own fantasy of disobeying all social conventions. The story ends with the two of them eating together in a park along the Dubai Creek, while he frantically and hopelessly tries to think of a way to get rid of her and go home to his wife.

The tone of the story is a strange blending of irony and compassion and humor. Al-Murr avoids all the easy ways that the story could go: the meaningful encounter with another lost soul, or the violent confrontation with an underworld far worse than his imaginings. There is no didacticism here, and no formula plot. But I see, or think I see, that the same respectability and concern for propriety that he thinks he has taken leave of for an evening are very much a part of his character. They are what spoil the evening for him as much as the outlandish behavior of the girl. Jasim himself doesn't see this. He only knows that he is miserable.

I read the story with a mixture of understanding and incomprehension. Al-Murr's irony is clear, and yet it seemed to me a flaw—or at least a source of confusion—that Jasim was such a flat character. I wanted to see his lack of self-awareness explored. I wanted to be sure of the shades of irony in which Jasim's double life was being drawn. I got most of it, I thought. Jasim's double life and his predicament at the end are both true and rather funny. But what else was there? I wasn't quite sure what was actually in the story, and what I was seeing in the story because of my own need to recognize familiar landmarks.

Another story, called "Problem and Solutions," is also an ironic little sketch that may have something more beneath its simple surface—and then again it may not. The central character in the story, Shamsa, is an unmarried schoolteacher in her early thirties, an old maid by Gulf standards. She is content with her single life but has no outlet for her gift of storytelling. So she amuses herself by making up shocking personal problems and submitting them to the advice columns of various newspapers. She writes about a woman who finds that the man she has married is really her long-lost brother, and receives the brisk reply that she needn't worry—their children are legitimate—but she and her brother must divorce and remarry other people as quickly as possible. This puzzles her a bit because she thought what she had described was a horrible calamity that would have ruined the lives of husband, wife, and children forever. How simple the advice writer can make things sound, she thinks, and she tries to devise a more complex problem that will surely leave him stumped. She writes another anonymous letter, this time about an adulterous wife who wants help in renouncing her sinful ways. Her evil alter ego receives a stern and sanctimonious rebuke in the paper's next edition. Again, sin is solved simply. All a person needs to do is stop it. Why doesn't everyone think of that? But she doesn't like the coldness of the reply and decides to devise a more sympathetic character for her next letter. She then writes in as a beautiful and wealthy widow who is pursued by many men and is afraid that she will be led astray. And to this, to her shock, she receives a personal response from Mr. Lonelihearts himself containing a marriage proposal and a picture of the fat balding man who has been solving all the problems of her imaginary people.

The plot is deft and funny. And yet, I again had the feeling of something missing when I read the story. I missed the richness of the specific, the groundedness that makes good contemporary American fiction work. I wanted to know more about Shamsa, about what she thought and felt. If I had received this story in a creative writing class, I would have told the student to flesh it out, to make it real. And yet, al-Murr's work is clearly not the work of a beginning writer. I was missing something. At the last roundabout, somebody must have turned the signs around.

In other stories, I saw other familiar landmarks, but I still wasn't sure whether I was headed in the right direction or interpreting what I saw to fit with where I hoped I was. I wanted to be in the middle of a good short story collection as much as I had wanted to be on the road to the grocery store. However, I wasn't sure whether the brown building on the left was the same brown building I'd passed earlier on my way to the grocery store or some other brown building on the way to Abu Dhabi. I often thought I was seeing social criticism along with the irony I knew was there, but I wasn't quite sure how accurate or deep this social criticism was, or exactly what was being criticized.

In the title story of the second collection, "The Wink of the Mona Lisa," a young man named Hasan "falls in love" with a young woman whom he sees at a wedding, one of the few occasions on which respectable young women could appear in public unveiled. But it isn't the girl's looks that fascinate Hasan at first, but the fact that the girl winks at him. She doesn't smile, she doesn't say anything to him, but she looks straight at him and winks. He admires her boldness and is thrilled that she has sought him out rather than just demurely waiting to be admired. Even though this girl isn't conventionally beautiful (the women in his family protest that the girl is really quite plain when he tells them of his interest), he begins to find her appearance more and more appealing. She has a mystery, a calmness, a beauty like that of the Mona Lisa, he tells his family.

He seems to be from a very traditional family and is determined to do things properly. Following proper Arab traditional courtship customs, he asks his mother to visit the girl's mother and find out if the girl's family would approve of an engagement. At first, both Hasan's mother and sisters object. The girl isn't really very pretty, they tell him, and although her family is perfectly respectable, they aren't the most prestigious. He could do better, they think. No, he insists. He must have that girl. Apparently, Hasan is something of a catch, because the girl's family readily agrees to the marriage and the girl herself makes no objection.

They marry and he finds the girl to be everything he imagined—gentle, calm, lovely in her own stately way—and with the secret streak of boldness that only he knows about but which he now imagines underlies her whole personality. After they have been quite happily married for several months, he confesses to her that it was her winking at him that first made him love her. She thinks back on the wedding at which he first saw her, tries to place the incident, and then remembers that was the night when she had an annoying speck in her eye and kept winking and blinking to try to get it out. But she doesn't tell this to her husband. Instead, she just smiles, and he remains quite happy with what he imagines is there.

I like the story not only for its craftsmanship, but also for its gentle and insightful social commentary, which validates the conventional wisdom of neither East nor West. To me, al-Murr is making gentle fun of the man for imagining himself to be in love with a girl with whom he has never even spoken. Because of the social traditions, he can't really know her personality and has to rely on his imagination, although he has no idea that this is what he is doing. And yet, the marriage is quite happy, which suggests the extent to which love can be a matter of imagining a personality for someone and falling in love with one's own fantasy. It doesn't matter that it isn't true. It's close enough. The story also calls into question the current "modern, Western" belief that a happy marriage must be based on honesty and a deep knowledge of the other person's character. Or am I imagining this subtext in the same way that Hasan read into his Mona Lisa's wink?

I wonder this about all the stories I like. To me, al-Murr's most interesting characters lead inner lives, but they are lives of fantasy rather than introspection. Al-Murr presents his characters from the outside, or records only their simplest responses. In this respect, they are quite unlike the characters in most contemporary English language short stories. I can make sense of al-Murr's technique, but I am not sure that it is the right sense. I can infer that these characters don't know themselves. Of necessity, they often have put up such a convincing conventional exterior for so long that they don't know who they are underneath—except that they are not who they pretend to be. For instance, it seems to me that in a sense Shamsa, the spinster letter writer, becomes the incestuous wife, the adulteress, and the tempted widow because they are not the self she enacts in her daily life. She invents these characters because they give her the sense of an existence outside her ordinary life. Jasim acts out a nighttime self that can't be part of his daily life because of social conventions, but he doesn't seem to understand that he is not really cut out for these sorts of escapades. The young bachelor seeks a mysterious girl who embodies his own fantasies of quiet rebellion, not knowing that what he seeks is a part of himself. To me, at least, these characters' problems and the apparent ironic wit with which both the characters and the problems are treated imply criticism of a society that demands such a degree of outward conformity.

Certainly, there is social criticism in some of the other stories, particularly those about women. Al-Murr depicts the sort of double standard that demands extremely circumspect behavior of women while allowing men considerably more latitude, as long as they don't make a public scandal. In a story called "Affairs of the Heart," a young woman named Aisha has had two traditional arranged marriages and was so abused by each of these men that she has sought and been granted divorces. One man was an alcoholic who beat her and flaunted his love affairs, and the other publicly insulted both her and her family. She has escaped from these horrible marriages, but because a respectable woman cannot live on her own, she lives with her uncle and his family. Unfortunately, although her uncle and his family treat her kindly, they don't really have room for her and her little girl, and she is forced to share a room with the maid. (It isn't clear why neither of her cousins offers to share a room with her, but it could be that they view her a bit as a poor relation rather than as an equal member of their family.) Next door to her uncle lives a young man about her age named Obaid, his widowed father, and his grandmother. Smitten by Obaid's charm and good looks, Aisha finds excuses to visit the grandmother, with whom she becomes friendly. She also develops an easy friendship with Obaid, bringing over his favorite dishes and joking with him about the forward young girls who call him on the phone to flirt with him. His father always treats her with formal respect. It seems to Aisha that in Obaid she has met a man who will treat her well. She knows Obaid's good nature and knows he would never insult her or beat her like her previous husbands, and yet, because they are neighbors and she is friendly with his grandmother, there can be no scandal attached to their acquaintance. After two failed arranged marriages, she at last has a chance to marry a man she actually knows and likes—no, loves. Finally, Obaid finds a chance to speak to her privately and makes a proposal. Unfortunately, it is not on his own behalf, but on his father's. Of course. It fits into place. A young man who has never been married would want to marry a young virgin, not a divorcee his own age. It is perfectly normal, however, for a middle-aged widower to marry a divorcee in her late twenties. After all, not many other people would. Aisha's options are limited. She cannot go on living with her uncle forever and Obaid's father is a decent man. Aisha tells Obaid to tell his father that she accepts.

It's a sad little story, well plotted, and moving in its compassion for a woman trapped by social conventions that deny her most elemental emotional needs while granting men the right to whatever private vices they choose. And I think this story and the others all tell me something about Emirati society. I can see, as al-Murr records, that these conventions are loosening so that standards of behavior that once applied to all men and women alike now apply only to some men and most women. Aisha can visit Obaid's house only under cover of being a neighbor and friend of the family, and yet younger women can phone him and flirt with him openly. Hasan goes through the traditional method of courtship in having his mother arrange his marriage for him, while Jasim can drive around the streets looking for women. Some of the women in al-Murr's Dubai are forced into loveless marriages, whereas other seemingly more liberated women have love affairs but are not necessarily any happier than the bored wives. I see the same thing, or think I do, when I pass the traditionally dressed couple in the shopping mall and then see the sophisticated young man and woman drinking in the hotel bar. And with al-Murr's help, I can imagine their worlds.

And yet, the stories that Emiratis are reading in Arabic

are not the same stories that I am reading in English, as I found out from discussing the stories with my students. I had been standing there poring over my map and peering at the street signs to figure out where I was—and then I finally figured out that the best way to get where I wanted to go was to ask someone local for directions. Again and again, the students told me that the stories that seem wryly ironic in English are hilariously funny in Arabic, particularly to Arabs from the Gulf. For one thing, they tell me, al-Murr has a wonderful ear for dialect. Many Arab writers follow the established convention of using standard literary Arabic even for dialogue. Only a handful of writers have their characters speak colloquial Arabic, which normally isn't even transcribed. It's apparently both surprising and very funny to see the inventive ways in which al-Murr transcribes Gulf Arabic. "You read the dialogue and then you laugh because you say to yourself, 'Yes, that's just how we would say it,' " one girl told me. "But I think that if a Lebanese or an Egyptian read these stories, he wouldn't understand them. It would be harder for them to understand the story in Arabic than it is for you to understand it in English." This might be an overstatement, but nevertheless, I think that much of the humor and insight comes from knowing the stories' social and linguistic context. I suspect that al-Murr is doing something like Faulkner does in *The Reivers,* where a character says "sour deans" for "sardines." Faulkner's phrase immediately struck me as amusing, as I think al-Murr's transcriptions do Gulf readers, both because the literal image is so bizarre and because that is exactly how the people I grew up with would have pronounced "sardines." I think that part of the reason the stories are so diverting to Gulf readers is that they are written in their own code.

They also find him funnier than I did because they are familiar with the social conventions that al-Murr's characters try to evade and with the equally customary methods for evading convention. The characters that sometimes seem so flat in the English translations may seem more rounded to Emirati readers because they are familiar with the type, and because they approach the stories less earnestly. Whereas I see Jasim as an insight into the modern Emirati man caught between tradition and modernity, my students see the jerk next door who gets exactly the punishment he deserves. They know Shamsa (she was probably one of their teachers in high school), they know the inane advice given out in the Arab newspapers' lonelihearts columns, and they are quite willing to believe that whoever is writing this advice must be pretty much a loser himself. And the stories are also funny because al-Murr is pointing out both the unspoken conventions and the unspoken methods for circumventing conventions.

My students laughed, for instance, at another story, "Bombay or Bust," in which a young Emirati couple go to Bombay thinking that they can enjoy a delayed honeymoon—dancing, holding hands in public, and doing all the things they can't do in public back home without damaging the woman's reputation. However, they find that their hotel is full of Emirati men, so the young wife grumpily eats room service meals alone while her husband fulfills his social obligations by going out to eat with the men.

To me, this seemed like a sad commentary on the strictness of the social conventions that deny people the most innocent enjoyments. But several of my women students found it very funny because, as one girl said, "Everybody knows this is exactly what would happen, but nobody else comes out and says it. We're all such hypocrites, really. We act one way at home and another way abroad, and everybody knows this." And yet, as she later admitted, hypocrite is really too strong a word. "We do it because we're stuck." In a way, I think, the laughter is a relief because someone has finally pointed out that the emperor has no clothes.

This explanation in part helped me to understand the lack of character development that I had previously found so troubling and which I had thought might be a deficiency in the writing. If a character is fully developed rather than a type, he often becomes sympathetic, and when a character is sympathetic, you can't laugh at him. Nevertheless, the explanation only really works for the stories that are clearly humorous or satiric. It doesn't explain the lack of character development in the more serious stories.

For this reason, I still feel somewhat ambivalent about al-Murr's style as it comes through in the English translations. A story such as "Affairs of the Heart" works only if one finds Aisha a sympathetic character. As it is, we pity her because of the plot and because of what we have been told about her in the exposition, but there is still a distance between her and the reader. Al-Murr's focus is on what happened, not on whom it happened to. A modern American writer, I think, would have individualized her and perhaps given the information about her previous marriages as a flashback. Developing the character would probably create a richer story in English, or at least a more familiar one.

It also seems to me that the literary short story might have evolved in a different direction in Arabic than in English. Obviously, plot can carry meaning as much as character can—as I see by looking at the late-nineteenth-century stories of

Guy de Maupassant and O. Henry, or at contemporary science fiction. The contemporary American short story, with its emphasis on detail and characterization, is not all the short story is or can be.

It also occurs to me that the richness and exactness of the language may make them better stories in Arabic than they are in English. My students have told me that the English stories were "simple and straightforward" and, they implied, a bit insipid. "They've lost all their flavor," one woman said. To me, the English prose seems worse than bland. It's clunky. The style is wordy, heavy on adjectives and adverbs, weak on exact verbs and nouns, and full of parenthetical phrases that disrupt the flow of thought. If the language were working with the stories rather than against them, I might not notice what now seem to be problems in characterization. The dips and bumps in the plot and characterization would be swept away by the flow of lovely words. Without being able to read Arabic, I can't tell if this is the fault of the text or of the translators, but I suspect the latter. Translators, after all, are scholars, not creative writers, and it is an unusual scholar who can write the kind of lively and graceful prose that would make these stories work in English.

Finally, what can a person tell about a society from fiction, and about fiction from its society? It may seem as if the answer is "Not much," but this isn't really true. I might have taken a few wrong turns, but I am very sure that I am in the United Arab Emirates, not the United States. On this level, it doesn't really matter if the stories are competently plotted ironic little sketches, as they seem in English, or good literary short stories, as I'm told they are in Arabic. They tell many of the things I want to know both about the Emirates and about its literary culture.

First, the stories themselves show me a culture in which the modern and the traditional exist side by side, often within the same people. But taken as a whole, the stories do not equate the modern with the corrupt and the traditional with the virtuous, but rather show that both good and bad have long been a part of the culture and that the present is in many ways an extension of the past. In both the past and the present, people lead conventional lives and fulfill their social obligations but yearn for something more, something else that they really can't define. Often, these people act foolishly. A few are spiteful and malevolent. Most, however, merely seem confused, primarily because they haven't given enough thought to who they are and how they should live their lives. However, while the characters may lack self-knowledge, the writer and the readers obviously do not, or they wouldn't find the characters' dilemmas so compelling and amusing.

And the phenomenon of al-Murr's work and its reception also reveals a great deal about the Emirates. What interests me particularly is that, unlike many postcolonial writers, al-Murr isn't writing for the Western market. He isn't trying to explain his culture and society to Western readers, as many serious third world writers do, nor is he attempting to present his society as curious and exotic, as so many of the second-rate writers do. What the Western reader thinks matters less than what the Gulf reader thinks. Al-Murr is speaking to other Gulf Arabs, and when I read the stories in English, I'm merely listening in on the conversation.

There seems to be a market here for stories and thought

and social criticism. Emiratis aren't just collecting government salaries and buying new cars and houses, as some westerners might think. Some Emiratis, at least, are finding it worthwhile to read fiction. Al-Murr is telling his audience what is wrong with their society and their attitudes. He tells them that they are too unthinking, that they put too much emphasis on the outward appearance of propriety while ignoring real moral values, and that they need more constructive outlets for their needs for excitement and creativity. And his readers are laughing and saying, "Yes, that's true."

Moreover, al-Murr isn't merely read here in the Emirates. He is promoted. His books are available in all the bookstores, and his stories are taught in the schools. This is a complete contrast to other Gulf states, particularly Saudi Arabia, where poets and essayists often find themselves in a great deal of trouble for suggesting that all is not perfect within the kingdom. (See Sadika Arebi's *Women and Words in Saudi Arabia.*) Of course, al-Murr's criticisms are social, not political, but this has not spared other Arab writers from persecution.

If al-Murr's stories are a map for me, they are a mirror to his countrymen, a fun house mirror reflecting people deformed by their vanities and fantasies. To use these stories as a map, I have to expand the focus to include not just the reflected image, but the actual people and their response to the reflected image. This complex and ambiguous truth is my map, a map that forms the face of a Mona Lisa who winks at me either because we share a secret or because she has a speck of dust in her eye.

PART THREE Looking Inward

Look to the blowing Rose about us—Lo,
Laughing, she says, into the world I blow,
At once the silken tassel of my purse
Tear, and its treasure on the Garden throw.

—The Rubaiyat of Omar Khayyam

The Garden and the Desert

When I came back to the Emirates in the summer of 1999, I was no longer coming to a strange place. I had traveled through the progression of months from September to June here before, feeling the temperature gradually drop and then rise again. In early October, the nights and early mornings would be cool enough for me to walk to my office, and then, slowly, the night air would become slightly chilly. The crested desert larks that had earlier sat on the railing of my window with their mouths open like panting dogs would be content to hop around the desert scrub outside my apartment. The migratory birds of southwest Asia would soon join them—brightly colored little birds that flitted among the flowering shrubs and trees of the newly built gardens. Every year, new ones would come, attracted by the flowers and insects that hadn't existed there just a few years before. By November, days would be cool enough to leave the air conditioning off, and then in February there would come nights when I would have to close the windows to keep out the cold. Then, the temperature would rise again, and it would be pleasant to sit outside at night for another month or so. By May, the daytime temperature would soar above one hundred again, the migratory birds would disappear, and my life would be enclosed within air-conditioned spaces again.

I was still in another country, but one that contained oases of familiarity. The landscapes I had walked and driven through became familiar even as they changed, because their changing had itself become familiar, not just the change of seasons, but the changes within the university campus and the cities that were coming closer to surrounding it. I had watched the bougainvilleas along the road between my apartment and office change from bare twigs to sturdy blooming bushes, and the little flame trees grow big enough to send out a few flowers. The open stretches of sand had turned into foundations of buildings and then into dormitories where the students in my classes lived. The students themselves became a little more disciplined, spoke English a little better. The departments were growing larger and more women—intelligent, articulate women who were active scholars and dedicated teachers—joined the faculty. The library was beginning to turn into a real university library where one could do research. The American University of Sharjah, with its gleaming polished marble plazas and domed buildings, no longer felt like a community college housed in the Taj Mahal, but a real university.

And yet, these changes seemed part of a natural order of things, like the change of the seasons. A garden of body and mind was springing up around me, but since I had been here to watch, it had come to feel as though its growth were part of my own.

Many times, as I looked out the windows of the faculty dining room or walked from the university gate to the edge of the desert, it seemed that the university was itself a metaphor.

Within the fence that surrounded the university, the world was green, with pink and purple patches of flower beds and splashing marble fountains. The sprinkler system drizzled down on the grass and left puddles like mirages on the tarred roads and brick sidewalks. Outside was the beige desert sand, dotted with gray-green dusty plants. The wind lifted and swirled the sand in a fine gritty mist, and the tufts of grass and the acacia trees sank deep roots looking for water in gravel-strewn sand that hadn't seen rain in a year. The desert plants were tough and enduring and had their own stark beauty. The grass and flowers were lush and fragile, and yet, walking along the flower-lined sidewalks tended by uniformed Indian gardeners, I would forget for a few moments how artificial this world was, only to be reminded again when dust swirled across the road.

It was easy to imagine that transforming world of the university as an Eden or paradise in the desert. It seemed both the fulfillment of an age-old dream that had grown out of the culture of the desert itself, and an artificial and foreign place that would shrivel and die in the barren vastness of the desert without water pumped in from outside. And yet, the gardens themselves were a way of seeing the world.

This desert had long had its own oases, clustered around springs and mountain valleys. Date palms and clover grew there, not flowers. And yet, contrast was central to both the idea of a garden and the idea of an oasis. The landscape was not unvarying, but full of difference. Contact with what was different was a familiar pattern. The people of the oases traded with the people of the desert and of the sea. The people of the sea traveled to other countries and cultures and back again. People didn't stay fixed. Change and contrast were a familiar pattern here, and contrast and change were becoming part of my own pattern of living.

Contrasts can exist side by side without either changing the other, and contrasts can intermingle until they form something new. The boundary between desert and garden was clear. But it reminded one always that something different was just outside. Inside the garden of the university, ideas sometimes commingled and sometimes stayed separate, but it seemed to me that the result of this kind of contact was always change. A person who rejects a different value or idea is still different from the person who imagines that everyone thinks as he does. The newly planted flowers and the migratory birds changed the ecology of the landscape in subtle and unpredictable ways, just as the people who passed through my life and those of the other people I came to know changed the ecology of the mind.

Wild and Tame

The Cheetah in the Bathroom

Tyger! Tyger! Burning bright
In the forests of the night,
What immortal hand or eye
Could frame thy fearful symmetry?

—William Blake

I was sitting in the veterinarian's office in Dubai with my cat when a man came in with a large hissing sack. All the other pets in the waiting room, yapping poodles and nosey labs alike, went silent and tried to hide under their owners' chairs.

The receptionist quickly motioned the man into a bathroom, and before the door closed, I saw him dump a groggy-looking spotted cat out onto the floor. It was not much bigger than a housecat, and I guessed it was one of the mixes of domestic and wildcats that I had read about—a domestic cat crossed with a spotted bobcat four or five generations back, giving it the markings and feral beauty of its wild ancestor without its temperament. I stood up to get a better look and its golden eyes met mine in a look that seemed both dazed and outraged before the vet and the owner closed the door.

"What kind of a cat was that?" I asked the receptionist.

"A cheetah," she told me, and then quickly turned back to her work.

I knew that cheetahs were an endangered species and that it must be illegal to import one to keep as a pet. But because the eastern Emirates share a seacoast with east Africa, smuggling wild animals in by sea must be fairly easy. The cheetah I had just seen was only a kitten, which explained why it was so small. Probably poachers had killed its mother to get it. It seemed cruel and childish to want to keep a cheetah, and yet part of me wished I could have one too.

I had once seen a fully grown leopard, in Sharjah, riding calmly in the passenger's seat of a little red convertible. (I don't think the car was a Jaguar, even though that would give the story more flair.) I was so startled that I missed my turn on the roundabout, and by the time I had both my car and myself under control again, the sports car and the big spotted cat were gone, and I was left wondering if I had somehow imagined what I thought I had just seen. I suspect that the animal's owner drove him around town to provoke just such a response. It was an astonishing and incongruous image, the high-tech beauty of the sports car and the savage beauty of the big cat, suddenly injected into the mundane world of people shopping and going to work as if no other world existed. It was an image of a powerful and dangerous world controlled, perhaps a misleading image. And yet, the image of the big spotted cat sitting in an open-top car as sedately as a human passenger delighted me.

The only other time I had seen a cheetah or a leopard at such close range was at the Sharjah Wildlife Center, a reasonably humane and beautifully designed zoo that was part of a desert museum about fifteen miles outside of Sharjah. The wildlife center was a little different than other zoos because it featured only animals that had once been native to the southern Arabian peninsula, and because the small animals and birds roved freely in a huge air-conditioned indoor garden, while the larger animals had half-acre outdoor runs landscaped to look like their native habitat. These runs looked roomy enough as I peered at them from the air-conditioned comfort of the indoor passenger walkways. The animals certainly had more space than the animals in the National Zoo in Washington, D.C. But for animals like the cheetah and the leopard that ranged over hundreds of square miles in the wild, the lot-sized habitats still must have felt like a cage. The cheetah must have longed to run. Curled up asleep just a few feet away from the glass partition and looking like an overgrown housecat, he looked at me with sleepy yellow eyes and then turned away—thinking what? That there was no point in trying to attack, because of the glass partition? That he had seen too many people in his life and was now tired of looking at them?

And now, I tried to consider why the sight of these beautiful and well-cared-for captive wild creatures made me feel not just awe at the power and beauty of the animal, or compassion for their lack of freedom (as I thought I ought to feel), but a profound excitement as well. I had seen big predators in the wild when I was a child growing up in the wooded hills of northwestern Pennsylvania, and I knew how I felt when there was no man-made partition between me and an animal that might view me as prey. Years ago, when I was barely a teenager, I was walking along a dirt road at night with a group of friends. We had been having a hayride, but the tractor that pulled the hay wagon broke down and we had to walk back to a friend's farm. Then we heard the chilling cry of a mountain lion not far in the distance, an eerie shriek that sounded almost like a woman's scream of terror and yet had a resonance and power that seemed not only inhuman, but unearthly. We all knew what it was. Several farmers in the area had found parts of sheep with their throats ripped out. All the clichés suddenly became real—my blood ran cold—an icy hand gripped my heart—my knees turned to jelly. Immediately the laughing and joking stopped, and we walked together in a tight little knot, hoping to see a car, a lighted farmhouse, anything that would remind us of our own safe world. Actually, we were probably safe because we were almost grown and in a group. A deer or a sheep would have been more tempting prey, although I am not sure what might have happened to a smaller child, alone. Nature is not gentle, and predators are predators. I think the thrill I feel at seeing a cheetah or a mountain lion now is the residue of that primordial fear.

Cheetahs had roamed the Arabian Peninsula well into the twentieth century, and in the mountains of the northern Emirates and Oman there were still a few Arabian leopards, smaller and paler than their African relatives. Both the Omani and Emirati governments were making heroic efforts to save the Arabian leopard from extinction, establishing wildlife preserves deep in the mountains. There was even an Arabian leopard at the wildlife center, nicknamed Arnold by the center's staff, whose handsome image adorned tote bags and sweatshirts in its gift shop. The Emirati government now has a very civilized relationship with the wild, viewing it not as something to fight against, but as something to be studied and conserved.

I can imagine what it must have been like, hundreds of years ago, when antelope and gazelles roamed the mountains and the oases. I can see the clumps of date palms around a wadi or spring, the antelope cropping the lush grass, moving nervously toward the cool tempting water, where the leopard waits to pounce, and I can see the cheetah galloping across the sandy plain after a herd of gazelles. It freezes into a tableau in my mind's eye, with the animals staring out at me as in Edward Hick's Peaceable Kingdom. But then the scene changes, and I can see a girl in a long dress come down to the spring to get water for her household, a girl like the one I saw on the isolated farm outside Hatta. A desert wind makes ripples on the water. The girl carries a big earthenware jug on her head. Carefully, she lowers the jug and then bends down to fill it with water. She can barely get the jug back onto her head again, for she is really still a child. The leopard is still there, just out of sight, as I continue to watch, horrified and fascinated.

There is, I think, something in many civilized urban people that loves wildness, but we want our danger made safe. In a world so controlled by human technology, it is possible to forget that life ends in death, that sudden death is part of nature, and that death is terrifying. Civilized man tries to create the illusion that death is something that we can control. I suppose that is also what the cheetah in the sports car suggests, or even the cheetah in his recreated habitat at the Sharjah Wildlife Center. Beautiful predators are not just what they are in themselves, but they become complex symbols whenever human beings view them, whether we see them as symbols of death or power or the untamed. We want to turn them into pets and trophies and mascots as a way of taming our own fears. And there is within us also a strong, perverse impulse not to tame the wild, but to let it do its worst—to let the cheetah out of the car, the zoo, or the vet's bathroom and watch what happens. We are both the predator and the prey, and the big cats remind of us all the amorphous and conflicting emotions of both.

Seeing them as symbols makes us cruel, even when we want to be humane. Perhaps the only way not to be cruel is to explore these symbols within ourselves, and to let the cheetahs and the leopards range in wildlife preserves far from any human settlement.

Someday, I like to think, I will be camping out in the desert. I will be with other people, but they will be asleep. Earlier, the outline of the jagged mountains loomed as black shadows in the distance, but now, the moon will have set and in the clear desert air I will be able to see every star in the Milky Way. The sand will be cool and rough under my hands as I lean back to look at the stars, or to watch the dying embers of the fire. Then far, far in the distance I will hear a sound I do not recognize at first—and then I will realize that is the cry of an Arabian leopard, the bark of a cheetah, the call of mortality, and I will feel the same fear that I did those many years ago. And yet, at the same time, I will know that for the time being, the cat and I are both safe, and I will accept that every part of nature, including myself, will die.

Distorted Images in the Mirror

The function of a wife seems to be to reflect a man's image back to him at twice its normal size.

—Virginia Woolf

When something unexpected happens in another culture, making sense of it is difficult because it's hard to tell the difference between something that is representative, that is, a fairly common occurrence that grows out of the culture and its dominant values, and something that is unusual. It is also tempting, when one first goes to another culture, to see what is unfair or unkind as representative, and what is humane as an individual act of kindness that happened in spite of the culture. Then, for me at least, after listening to other westerners' racist comments about Arabs, it becomes easy to generalize in the opposite direction and to dismiss real problems too readily. In the foreign society that we view and criticize, we see a distorted version of our own society, with our own society's concerns made central even if they are not particular issues to the people within that culture. Perhaps, rather than hope to become a truly objective observer, the best that a person can do is to try to avoid being a mindless critic or apologist. Instead, one can try to learn as much as possible about a society from people who live in that society, knowing that something will still be left out and that what one can understand best is the process of one's own mind trying to understand. We can look at the distorted image, knowing it is distorted, and knowing that part of the distortion comes from a desire to see a greater image of ourselves, either by imagining ourselves to come from a superior culture or by imagining ourselves to be less prejudiced than our countrymen.

When I am tempted to generalize too glibly, I remember the story once told to me by a Chinese woman from Singapore who was studying in the United States. She had been to a rather rowdy fraternity party, and in the course of the evening, a boy had poured a glass of beer over a girl's head when she refused to dance with him. The Chinese woman expected the boy to be thrown out of the party immediately, perhaps even arrested. But instead, nothing happened. The girl burst into tears and ran off to the bathroom to dry her hair, and the rest of the crowd just laughed, to the extent that they even noticed. And soon the beer-dosed girl herself returned to the party and acted as if nothing had happened. "I had a difficult time understanding this American custom," the Chinese woman told me, "because in my country that would be considered very rude."

And how could I begin to explain to her that it was considered very rude in my country, too, when she had seen the opposite with her own eyes? She had already come up with an elaborate explanation: incidents like this were part of what Americans meant by individualism. In America, it was everyone for himself, and everyone did whatever he could get away with. If you couldn't take care of yourself, then tough luck. America was essentially a country without norms of civil behavior, she'd decided. The incident had obviously disturbed her, and she had come up with an explanation that fit in with what she had read about America and seen in American movies. Her explanation was logical and even had a germ of truth within it. I'm also sure she was quite right that the incident wouldn't have been the same if it happened in Singapore. The only problem was that her explanation wasn't true, primarily because of the limits of her knowledge about America.

I tried to keep this story in mind when I sought to understand two incidents that took place during my first and second year in Sharjah. One of the incidents showed a more humane aspect of Emirati society than most Americans would expect, and the other seemed to confirm some of the stereotypes that Americans have about the Middle East, and yet showed, I think, the ways that stereotype is a distortion. Both of these events unfolded differently than they would have in the United States, and therefore might illustrate some of the differences between the societies. Both concern the treatment of women or children; both concern people who were outside the society, although to differing degrees. How a society treats its most vulnerable people, I think, reveals more than how the average citizen lives, and thus the two stories, while not necessarily representative, do reflect an image of Emirati society, if we learn how to correct for the distortion.

The first incident involved my new colleague Leona and her teenage son Adam, both intelligent and open-minded people who were trying to learn about the society around them. They had just come to the Emirates from Georgia, and for both of them, it was the first time they had traveled outside the United States, much less lived in a non-Western culture. And so despite their openness, they came with some of the preconceptions about Arabs that most Americans share. They'd seen movies where the villains were Arab terrorists and watched television documentaries about Arab misogyny, and while Leona and Adam were skeptical people, these American-made images at first superimposed themselves on the real people around them. The distortions were in the American lens through which they were accustomed to seeing the world.

As Leona came to know her Arab and Arab American colleagues, she began to examine these stereotypes, and when she met Western business people in Dubai who told her what Arabs thought and felt, their comments about Arabs were so similar to what the good old boys back in Georgia said about African Americans that she shrewdly inferred that the generalizations came from the same mindless bigotry. To a degree, at least, AUS was a liberal American enclave in the midst of both foreignness and hostility to foreignness, a refuge when local behaviors and those of our fellow Americans got on our nerves. And because Leona was a conscientious teacher, teaching Arab students also made it easier to examine at closer range and in more detail what had looked so true from the distance of America. If she didn't always like or understand what she saw, her affection for her students blurred the cutting edges.

Her son Adam, however, was plunged into the middle of a Middle Eastern society, a society of middle-class teenagers from all over the region, most of whom were living away from their extended families and thus were removed from many of their own traditional values. He was attending an "American" high school in Sharjah, but he was the only American in his class. The rest were Arabs, Iranians, and Indians whose parents wanted them to learn English better than they would in the local government schools. Although he was a bright boy anyway, the fact that English was his native language helped to put him at the top of his class—and made many of his classmates want him to let them copy his homework and give them the answers to exams. Probably, they did this because they were under pressure to succeed academically in a language with which they weren't comfortable, and the cheating was for many an act of desperation.

Knowing this, however, wasn't helpful to Adam, who still had to decide what to do about friends who wanted him to help them cheat, or to Leona, who saw her son growing more and more contemptuous of the ethics of his Arab friends. He solved his problem by dropping the friend who had been most insistent, a local boy named Hassan. This was a mature and reasonable decision, I thought. And since it wasn't my problem, I didn't give it much more thought until a few months later, when Leona told me about what had just happened to Adam.

Early in the evening, Adam had gone out to visit one of his friends, an American boy who played on his baseball team. Leona had gone to bed early, unaware that the friend's parents kept a well-stocked liquor cabinet and were out for the evening. In Dubai, alcohol is legal for non-Muslims as long as they buy a liquor license, but in Sharjah, where we lived, alcohol is illegal for anyone, and public drunkenness is a crime that can land a person in jail. And in the eyes of Muslims, of course, it is also a sin, which was part of why my students were so distressed by the girl's drinking in the Alice Munro short story. I suppose they view drinking rather like conservative Americans view drug use—as something both illegal and immoral that threatens the traditional values of the society.

Part of what happened next is quite predictable. The boys helped themselves to the liquor, and being unused to drinking, Adam didn't realize the difference between just enough and far too much until the room turned into a merry-go-round. Realizing only that he felt very sick and wanted to go home, he called a cab and asked the driver to take him back home. Then he passed out before explaining exactly where home was. The driver tried to rouse Adam to get directions, but Adam was still out cold.

This created a definite problem for the driver, an Indian guest worker. He had a drunken American teenager passed out in his back seat and nowhere to take him. So he apparently decided to ignore the problem as long as possible and continued to drive around Sharjah for the next several hours, picking up fares and, I suppose, hoping that Adam would wake up and tell him where to drive. I imagine that the various passengers that evening couldn't have been pleased about getting into a taxi that smelled like a brewery and having to ride in the front seat, but apparently no one made a fuss about it.

However, when it got to be past midnight and the driver's shift was over, he was forced to confront his problem. He still had a drunken boy sleeping in his back seat, he didn't know what to do with the boy, and he hadn't been paid. So he drove to the police station, took his fare from Adam's wallet with the police watching, and let the police decide what to do with him.

According to the law, what they should have done with him was to arrest him immediately for public drunkenness, a fairly serious crime. But they did not. They took him into the station, made him drink coffee, and tried to find out who he was and where he lived. Because the police didn't speak much English, and Adam didn't know any Arabic and was only marginally coherent, they started looking through his address book. There they found the name and phone number of his exfriend Hassan, who came from a fairly prominent local family, and called him. It was now about 1:00 A.M. Fortunately, the boy's older sister was awake, and she and her husband were willing not only to vouch for him but to come down to the police station. She called Leona and explained the situation, but also explained that everything was "taken care of." There would be no charges. The police would drive Adam home. She and her husband would come with them. "We explained to them that Adam was a good boy but he made a mistake, and they just said, 'Boys make mistakes sometimes,' " she told Leona.

And that was the end of it. Or almost. Leona was shocked to discover that Adam still had his entire allowance with him, except for the hundred dirhams (about thirty-five dollars) that the taxi driver had taken for driving him around Sharjah all night.

"We had a long talk about all of this as soon as he woke up," Leona told me. "And after I had yelled at him for being so stupid and irresponsible and told him that he wasn't in the United States any more where you can be an idiot and get away with it, I suddenly realized that he had gotten away with it. When I got that phone call, I had visions of something like *Midnight Express*, but that didn't happen. I don't know why. I remember I told him that he might sneer at the Arab kids and their cheating, but if he had gotten drunk in the U.S.

and ridden around in a cab half the night, he wouldn't still have his money in his billfold, and some woman he hardly knew wouldn't have gone down to the police station in the middle of the night to keep him from getting into real trouble."

I had seen bits and pieces of the movie *Midnight Express,* which was about a young American man imprisoned and brutalized in Turkey for drug smuggling. The film was so violent and so disturbing that I hadn't been able to watch the whole thing. I had also read Cormac McCarthy's brilliantly written and horrifying novel *All the Pretty Horses,* the story of a group of American boys imprisoned in Mexico. The message from both popular and high American culture seemed to be that young Americans who stepped outside the law in foreign countries could expect neither justice nor humanity, almost as if the very concept of decency were uniquely American. The foreign culture in both cases was a mirror in which American culture was reflected at twice its real size. And yet, Leona and Adam both saw that this easy assumption was far from true; in fact, the opposite was true. The monster mask in the mirror was a twisted reflection of a more benign face than they might have encountered at home.

What happened to Adam wasn't merely good luck, but an outgrowth of the society in which it happened. For one thing, while Hassan's older sister was clearly a very nice woman, I don't think she was merely being kind. She was also exercising her family's *wasta. Wasta* is usually translated as "influence," but that doesn't begin to suggest the complex system of reciprocal favors that operates both outside of and in conjunction with the legal system of many Arab countries. There is an official rule or law. And then there are ways around that law if you happen to know someone. It may sound as if *wasta* is simply a form of corruption, and this is certainly how many westerners respond to it. But *wasta* is usually just a way of cutting through bureaucracy in ways that don't harm anyone and that enhance the prestige of the person who is able to exercise the *wasta.* It is a system of patronage, I think, in which those who have *wasta* are almost obliged to exercise it on behalf of the less powerful. Thus it didn't really matter that Hassan and Adam had quarreled. The boy needed help, and the sister felt an obligation to use her *wasta* with the police to help him out.

I also think that the police didn't particularly want to arrest Adam. That is why they looked through his address book and called a local family before they called his mother. It seems to me that they were looking for an excuse not to arrest Adam, and a local family's intervention was a very good reason. They didn't really want to arrest him because they could see that he was just a boy, and their society—to the extent that one can make these sorts of generalizations—gives a certain amount of leeway to children and their lapses in judgment. Some of those policemen might have had imperfect children of their own, and although they may have seen the offence as greater than most Americans would, they could also see that no one had been harmed by this escapade. They were willing to be lenient when they could have been harsh not only because they were kindly, but because the informal structure within the society supported their generous impulse.

I don't want to make more of this incident than is there, or to see a whole culture in one event. Certainly, if the incident had happened in Saudi Arabia, it probably wouldn't have had such a happy ending. Yet it did happen in the Emirates, and that in itself not only contradicts a stereotype but makes one think more about American society and how we view both legality and foreignness. If Adam had passed out in public in a small American town, the local police might have responded in just the same way, especially if they knew Adam and his family. Adam might even have fared as well if he had been taken to a couple of policemen on patrol in a big city, although probably not if he were actually taken to the station. But in Sharjah, drinking is a far more serious offence than underage drinking is in the United States, and Adam's problems were compounded by his being a foreigner. I'm not sure that Americans would have been as likely to react as generously, and as illegally, if a drunk foreign teenager who didn't speak any English were brought to an American police station in the middle of the night. What distorts the image may well be a reflection of ourselves.

What interests me most, however, was that no one involved in the incident seemed to be concerned with laws or rights. This may have been just as well, since Adam had broken the law and didn't have any rights other than to a trial before a Sharia judge. Instead of seeing it in terms of laws and rights, everyone involved seemed to view it as a matter of children and adults, and the immediate concern of all the adults, from the driver to the police to the sister, seemed to be "How do we get this boy home?" Everyone played a role in circumventing the law, taking care only not to get into trouble himself. No one said, "The law is the law and it must be upheld." In any culture, I think, there is a difference between what is officially true and what actually happens, and one doesn't know a culture until one has seen, many times, what really happens. From what my students had written again and again in their personal experience essays, it seemed as if what happened to Adam was not an anomaly, but the norm. Teens who did stupid and illegal things—drag racing, vandalism, petty theft, fighting—were usually let off with a warning as long as their crimes didn't involve serious violence.

The other incident that made me re-examine the meaning of the American images of the Middle East was more complex, because it involved a girl rather than a boy. It is very difficult to write truthfully about the lives of Middle Eastern women because westerners so often see their situation as a plight and interpret the restrictions placed on women as the result of misogyny and patriarchy. It's patronizing and a bit hypocritical to say that Emirati women have a plight—hypocritical because focusing on the mistreatment of Arab women gives us an excuse to ignore the far more oppressive mistreatment of the Palestinians, for instance. And far from being hated or disvalued, women in the Emirates tend to be sheltered and often cherished. Yet they are not free to make their own choices in the way most Western women are, although it is difficult to say this without seeming to give credence to all the stereotypes.

I realized some of the complexity of the status of young women when Shaima, a lively Emirati girl, came by my office to tell me she was getting married.

"Congratulations," I said.

"Don't say that," she told me. "I don't want to get married yet. I want to finish my schooling first. But my cousin has proposed to me and my aunts want me to accept him. My mother thinks it is a good match, but she is crying all the time because she thinks I am too young and she doesn't want to lose me. They tell me he is a good man with a good career and that he will give me a happy life." She spoke mechanically, as if reciting a memorized speech, and then suddenly her eyes filled with tears.

"What does your father say?" I asked.

"My father died three years ago. I told you that before, professor," she pointed out. I had forgotten. "But I don't think my father would have agreed to this marriage."

Reminded, I began to recall the other things she had told me about her life. Her mother was a Lebanese who had married a local man and now lived as a widow in Abu Dhabi with her husband's family. Shaima herself lived in Dubai with her aunt and uncle, another branch of her father's family, while she was attending the university. I am not sure who was paying her tuition, but I guessed that with the death of her father, Shaima and her mother had gone from being members of a wealthy family to being poor relations.

"He's a good man in many ways," she went on, brushing aside her tears and trying to smile. "He says I can finish university if I want and then I can work with him in his company." I wondered if this meant that he would take over the tuition payments, which weren't cheap.

"Do your aunts know you don't want to get married?"

"I've told them I want to finish my education first, but they don't think I should miss this chance. I can't tell them I don't want to marry him. They'll think I'm saying their boy isn't good enough for me, or they'll think I have fallen in love with some boy I've met here." The latter, I knew, would be scandalous to a traditional family, as her father's seemed to be. Moreover, Lebanese like Shaima's mother were sometimes less socially conservative, which might have had her father's family worried.

"Can't he wait until you've finished university?" I asked.

"He's twenty-seven. He says he doesn't want to wait any longer to get married."

Shaima was seventeen. In her papers that first semester, she had written about the excitement of living away from home and meeting people on her own, even if it were only her teachers and classmates in college. Now, after that taste of independence, that part of her life was over. I almost wished she would run away, as Laila had.

And yet, I couldn't say any of this to her. There was nothing I could do to change the circumstances of her life, and saying anything that would make her more discontent than she already was wouldn't help her. So I just said, "Well, maybe it will all turn out better than you think now."

"Insha'allah," she said. "This is my fate and I have to accept it."

She was married at the end of the semester, and when I came back at the end of the summer, Shaima was in my class again. But she seemed different. She still made intelligent comments in class, and her work was still good. But she came late to almost every class, often missing the quizzes I gave to make sure students read the assignment. Some days she missed entirely. After about a month of this, she came to my office to explain the reason. She was pregnant and suffering from severe morning sickness.

"I thought you wanted to wait awhile until you had a baby," I remarked.

"I did," she said. "But God had other plans for me." And she went on to explain that she had heard that if a woman used birth control before she had her first child, she would have difficulty getting pregnant later. She also told me that her mother-in-law wanted her to quit school, telling her that overwork was likely to harm both her and her baby. When she finally told them that she would drop out for one semester, during the late months of her pregnancy, her mother in law had bought her a gold necklace.

"And when I told her I was going to come back to the university after the baby was born, she said she wanted to take it back," Shaima told me with a laugh.

"It's going to be harder, with a baby," I said. "But women do it all the time. When I was in Saudi Arabia, a lot of girls like you finished university even after they had children." And then, remembering that English-speaking Arabs usually only used "girl" to refer to unmarried women, I added, "I mean young women like you."

"Ah," Shaima said, "I miss that girl, professor. I liked being that girl."

I missed that girl too, and I wanted to understand what happened to her. If I told other Americans about Shaima, they would tell me that this was how Arab society treated women, because women had no rights in the Arab world. The truth, I think, was more complex. Shaima was married at seventeen and a mother at eighteen because she was caught in a web of complex social and legal forces that sometimes acted as a safety net but in this case acted as a snare. The older women in her family thought they knew what was best for her better than she herself did, or at least they had that pretext. In fact, they may have arranged the marriage because it was easiest for them. It was contrary to Islamic law to force a girl to marry against her will, and yet Shaima had married a man she didn't want to marry because to actually object would have meant to alienate the family who were taking care of her. Force was forbidden, but pressure was not, and in practice they amounted to the same thing. Usually the parents rather than the extended family made decisions about when a girl married, and a girl's finishing her education was considered a legitimate reason for not marrying by all the Arab families I knew. Shaima's father was dead, however, and her mother's wishes had less weight than they usually would because she was a foreigner.

Shaima also had no way of being financially independent. She had the social status of an upper-class girl but no money of her own. She couldn't work at any of the kinds of jobs that an American woman might to finance her way through school. She couldn't be a clerical worker or a saleswoman—her family's social status would not allow this; and besides, in the Emirates these jobs were filled by Filipinas and Indians, not women from the Gulf. In fact, she couldn't work without her family's permission anyway, which meant that whatever independence working might give a woman, independence from her family was not included.

What had happened to Shaima wasn't the norm, but it was not uncommon either, and it seemed to me that it shouldn't even have been possible. When I talked to Arab women about it, they also condemned it, which I think is significant in itself. "Her aunts are bitches," one woman told me. "They don't want to have to support her and they don't want her going around besmirching their family name, so they've married her off while she's still like a blind kitten."

Perhaps so. Whether the aunts were selfish or merely misguided, the social structure gave her aunts a great deal of power and Shaima very little. They had this power because so much of a family's social standing rested on the reputations of the women. The aunts' reputations for respectability were already well established, whereas Shaima's was questionable, not because of anything she herself had done but because she was young and unmarried. If people talked about Shaima, it affected the whole family, which was why the family assumed the right to make collective decisions for individual people.

Shaima was being provided for. She would live the life of an upper-class woman with material comforts and a considerable measure of security. She would have the self-esteem that came from knowing she came from a reputable family and had acted with propriety, and because of her family's unsullied reputation other Gulf families would treat her with respect.

None of this made what happened to Shaima less unfair. Although in fact the cousin seemed like a perfectly nice man, no one would have cared if he flirted with girls as long as he wasn't involved in some blatant public scandal; only Shaima's behavior mattered. He could choose whom he wanted to marry; she couldn't. In many ways, she seemed like the trapped women in Mohammad al-Murr's short stories.

And yet, and yet. One of the effects of living in the Middle East was that I not only saw customs and values different from my own, but I also had an idea of how the West looked to some Arabs. And to many Arab men and women I had spoken to, America did not look like a paradise for women. I remembered bits and pieces. I remembered teaching *The Sound and the Fury* to graduate students in Saudi Arabia, and the remark of an Egyptian girl who was also Muslim fundamentalist. We had been discussing the dysfunctional Compson family, and more particularly, the sister Caddy, whom one critic had described as possessing every virtue except chastity.

"But can she be blamed for that?" the girl had said. "Her father thinks that all women are weak and ignores her and only cares about Quentin, and her mother never shows her any love either—all the mother's love goes to Jason. Her father treats her mother with total contempt, and the mother whines and complains and pretends to be sick. Is it any wonder Caddy turns to sex to try to find the affection she never found at home? How can she have any self-respect when no one has ever treated her with respect or acknowledged her virtues?" She paused, and then went on. "Isn't that what often happens in America, that girls experiment with sex when they are really still children because their families don't make them feel that they are valuable? I'm not sure if this is true of an adult, but when a girl is still in her teens like this, doesn't a great deal of her self-respect come from how her family treats her? I know her father is supposed to be a sympathetic character, but I just hate him for what he has done to his daughter."

And I thought about what a Saudi graduate student I knew in the United States had told his wife when she wanted to return to Saudi Arabia by herself. Away from her family for the first time in her life and knowing no English, she was lonely and miserable. The only other Arabic-speaking woman in the small town was an Egyptian graduate student who snubbed her, and it wasn't proper for her to talk to men. She didn't know how to drive and her husband wouldn't teach her, so she was stuck in their small apartment all day with no one to talk to. Of course she wanted to go home.

"Go ahead and go home," her husband told her. "I can get an American girlfriend to come and live with me. She'll sleep with me and take care of the house and she'll be grateful if I don't ask her to pay half the rent. I can throw her out whenever I want and there's nothing she can do about it. The police aren't going to arrest me for living with a woman I'm not married to. Her parents aren't going to complain if I live with her and then kick her out. Women don't have any rights here and their families don't protect them. So go home if you want to. I'll have a good time." And unfortunately, he was probably right. I knew of several women graduate students who stayed with abusive boyfriends in part because they couldn't afford places of their own. There probably were many American women who would move in with a married man whose wife was away, especially if he were financially generous, as this man could afford to be. To both students, it was the American society, not their own, that abused and exploited women. Was the image of Arab misogyny really a way of avoiding an examination of the extent to which our society is patriarchal and misogynist? Certainly, American women usually had choices that many Arab women did not, and yet there was truth in what the Arab graduate students had said. Without financial security, a woman's choices are limited no matter where she lives, and without emotional security, it can be hard to make choices that are not self-destructive.

It was good to keep this in mind, but more important to remind myself that just as their view of the status of women in American society was incomplete, so was my view and perhaps any westerner's view of the status of women in Arab societies. Living in another culture often reminds me that the only truth I know is a fictive truth, a subjective truth that comes from the interaction of who I am and what I have seen. When I return to my own society once more, I try to piece the bits of reality I have encountered into a pattern, a pattern made up of not only pieces of other societies, but pieces of mirror as well, so that when I look at the mosaic I will see not only fragments of difference, but also reflections of myself and the cultures that shaped me.

Windows into America

Of the four billion people in the world, three and three fourths billion are not Americans. But Americans don't seem to know this.

—student paper

In September of 1998, the university sponsored an "intercultural seminar" in which American teachers and Arab teachers were supposed to exchange views and increase their understanding of one another's cultures. This idea was very nice in theory, but it unfortunately presupposed that both westerners and Arabs had only one viewpoint per group. Moreover, most of the activities were organized by American teachers who themselves had only a superficial understanding of Arab societies. The result was that many Arabs and westerners came away from the seminar with their stereotypes confirmed rather than challenged.

I don't think I myself came to understand much more about Arabs from this encounter, and yet I did gain some insights into Americans and myself from the discussion and from my efforts to understand, later, exactly what went wrong. I vividly remember one young woman librarian explaining her shock at the way non-Americans responded to her. "I thought people liked Americans," she said. "Or at least I thought they would like us once they got to know us. But they don't. They like American music and movies, but they don't like us and they don't like it when I try to talk about American values. Yes, I know the stereotype of the ugly American, but nobody I know goes around slapping people on the back and saying, 'How much is that in real money?' I keep thinking, 'What's not to like about us?' " Immediately, several of the Arab teachers on the panel reassured her that they liked her, and indeed thought she was "very sweet." The American woman looked flustered because, I think, she was asking an honest question, not seeking personal reassurance, but her train of thought was broken and she said no more.

As I thought about the incident, I saw several levels of misunderstanding going on. The Arab teachers might have thought they knew what an American was. In this case, they might have thought it meant an extremely naïve person who couldn't distinguish between other people's reactions to American foreign policy and their reactions to her personally. Or they might have thought it meant a person who was so unthinking that she actually believed her government's self-serving rhetoric despite ample evidence that American actions and American rhetoric don't always match. Her innocence may have seemed like the kind of false innocence that comes from refusing to examine one's actions and beliefs, and indeed, of never feeling the need for such self-examination. They might not have disliked her personally, but they certainly disliked the values they thought she embodied. That was why they treated her like a child and why the young woman was so embarrassed.

I think I understand why they may have felt that way. A

hundred years ago, Arabs who were educated in colonial schools had learned quickly that noble sentiments such as "fair play" and "liberty, equality, and fraternity" did not apply to the European powers' relations with their colonial subjects. American government rhetoric about democracy and human rights sounds like more of the same, especially when one considers not only American foreign policy toward the Middle East, but the anti-Arab tone of so much of American public discourse. Western-educated Arabs are very aware of both, and it is a constant source of resentment. It was small wonder then that the Arabs whom the librarian met were so skeptical when an American started talking about American values.

Nevertheless, their patronizing dismissal of her question disturbed me. I think that the young woman was trying to understand the world around her and that she had the courage to ask questions rather than assuming that she knew all the answers. She seemed willing to change her opinions as she learned new things, and to question what she thought she knew. In this respect, she embodied what is best about Americans. Her openness, however, also made her a much easier target than the ignorant, arrogant, and powerful American of the stereotype. If she had the courage to keep asking, she would find out what was not to like about Americans, and she could struggle to avoid becoming that kind of American herself. But her Arab colleagues hadn't made her journey an easier for her.

Years ago, when I first read James Baldwin's essay, "The Discovery of What It Means to Be an American," I didn't fully understand why he had to leave the country to learn what being an American meant, perhaps in part because I was envious of his opportunity to live in Paris. I was also a bit skeptical when he quoted Henry James's statement that being an American was a complex fate. How was being American more complex than being German or Chinese, for instance? The observation struck me as chauvinistic. But after living in the Middle East off and on for almost twenty years, I was beginning to understand why being an American is not only complex, but difficult, and why it might be easier to understand this difficulty when one sees Americans interacting with people who are not like them.

A person doesn't have to go outside the United States to realize that beliefs in democracy and human rights are not uniquely American, or that American foreign policy is often determined by self-interest rather than idealism. But I have needed years of living outside the United States and seeing how foreigners react to Americans, and of observing how Americans respond to foreigners both within and outside the United States, to realize that the problem is not just one of a government that doesn't always live up to its high-minded rhetoric, nor of boorish American travelers. The problem is with the attitudes of many educated Americans.

This problem was illustrated for me both in Sharjah and earlier, in the United States, when I witnessed two incidents that disturbed me deeply and that I might not have been attuned to if I had not lived outside the United States. They were not isolated incidents, I think, but part of a pattern, not of hypocrisy, precisely, but of unquestioned assumptions.

A Window to Freedom of Expression

A few months after the intercultural seminar, an Arab American colleague of mine named Hani began to publish opinion pieces—op-eds—in one of the local English language newspapers. Although Hani was originally Iraqi, he risked arrest if he returned to Iraq because of his opposition to the Ba'ath regime. After many years of living in the United States, he had become an American citizen. He had family in Iraq, however, to whom he was sending much of his paycheck. This income, at least, enabled them to buy food. As his wife pointed out to me, food was available in Iraq, but it cost more than ordinary Iraqis could afford. Two pounds of meat would cost a week's salary for a high school teacher. Iraqis who did not have support from family working outside the country simply starved in a man-made famine in the midst of plenty. It was not surprising, then, that although Hani was against the Iraqi regime, he was also against the U.S.-led sanctions and wanted to write about this in the local English newspapers, where he would be read by other Americans. He also strongly opposed the U.S. air strikes that began in December 1998 and killed scores of people who had nothing to do with determining the Iraqi government's policies. In one of his op-eds, he voiced his objections to the air strikes and suggested that they would lead to a rise in anti-Americanism throughout the Middle East. American interests throughout the Middle East were likely to become targets, he said. In this, he was simply echoing the warnings that all Americans in the Emirates had received from the American embassy.

He was right about the rise in anti-American sentiments. Some of my normally apolitical students began writing their freshman essays about the cruelty and unfairness of attacking an undefended country, and, echoing what they had read in Arabic language newspapers (I had told them they had to cite their sources) rather simplistically declared that Clinton had ordered the air strikes to distract American public attention from the Monica Lewinsky scandal. From what I could gather from my students and from Arabic-speaking faculty members, both Emirati and imported Arabic newspapers were vehement in their criticism of the air strikes and cynical about the air campaign's timing and motivation.

When Hani's article came out, I was pleased at first. I had known many Arab Americans who criticized U.S. foreign policy toward the Middle East among themselves, but never made any effort to explain their views to other Americans. I used to tell them, "How do you expect American policy to change if you don't tell people why it's wrong? The only people you talk to are people who already agree with you. What good does that do?" I was very happy to see someone who had the courage to publish his views instead of just becoming cynical and bitter. I also thought it was good publicity for the university, since some local people might fear that an American-style university was really intended to indoctrinate Arab students. Hani's op-ed, I thought, made it clear that there was a range of opinion among Americans at the university, and better still, it showed that Americans were free to criticize their country's policies. What better way to demonstrate, I thought, that Americans really did value freedom of expression? Unfortunately, I was painfully naïve in my assumptions.

Before Hani's article, little of the criticism of the air strikes had appeared in the English-language Emirati papers, and many of the American faculty members assumed that the

Emiratis supported the U.S. policy. And apparently some Americans who didn't know Hani assumed that he was an Iraqi, not an American. I am afraid that others who knew he was an Arab American simply mentally omitted the "American" whenever someone who was not of European origin criticized American policy. Thus, when Hani warned of possible attacks on U.S. interests in the Middle East, some faculty members, including one of the deans, interpreted the article as calling for attacks on Americans. This wasn't a very logical assumption, because if Hani had wanted to incite his fellow Arabs to attack his adopted countrymen, he would have written his articles in Arabic and published them in Arabic newspapers where other Arabs would read them. The only people who read the English language newspapers were British and American expats, and English-educated Indians, who were very apolitical, at least about Arab politics. Even most of the Arab students at AUS, who read English fairly well, preferred reading the Arabic newspapers because they felt more comfortable with them both linguistically and culturally.

Fear can overcome logic, however, and I can understand the fear of the American faculty members, to some extent, since American embassies and military installations in the Middle East have been bombed. When one is frightened, it is difficult to bear in mind that no one had been attacked in the Emirates and that American universities had never been targeted. Yet fear cannot account for all that happened.

I expected academics who were upset with what a colleague had written to do one of two things. They could have talked to Hani about his article and asked him what he meant. When I was teaching in the United States, I had a running debate with a Jewish colleague about the op-eds I wrote during the Gulf War, and after a while our talks became interesting and exciting. At the time Hani published his articles, the American University of Sharjah was a small school with only about a hundred faculty members. It would have been very easy for anyone to stop by Hani's office or send him an e-mail to ask him what he meant. But no one did. Colleagues who didn't feel comfortable speaking to Hani personally could also have written their own op-eds or letters to the editor explaining why they disagreed with Hani's opinions and refuting his arguments. They didn't do that either.

But the problem wasn't merely that American academics of European ancestry failed to treat an Arab American as colleague. I suppose I shouldn't have been shocked when the university stopped the articles. After a few days of hearing rumors, the faculty received a memo stating that any article that a faculty member wrote for the local media should first be approved by a faculty media committee, and that the local press had been instructed not to accept any work by AUS faculty unless it had media committee approval. The dean of our college, who didn't agree with this decision, also called Hani to his office and told him privately that the university had asked the editor of the opinion page not to accept any more of his work. Later, Hani told me that he had pointed out to the dean, another Arab American, that none of the local Arabs had objected to what he had written. Why should they? It was no different than what they had been reading in the Arab press for weeks. But according to Hani, the dean also told him that if Americans in the administration objected to what Hani was writing, he was going to have to stop writing, because the goodwill of important Americans at the university was more valuable to the administration than what an Arab American assistant professor might have to say.

The event disturbed many people on the faculty, but not in the way I thought it would.

"They're taking advantage of the fact that there isn't any free press here to shut him up," a friend of mine said.

"They're not used to freedom of expression here," another American colleague said. "And after all, it's their country, not ours. We don't have any right to force our ways on them. If they don't like freedom of expression, why make a big deal about it."

"You've got to admit that Hani is a loose cannon," a friend in the English department told me. "We can't have him running around writing those inflammatory essays. You've got to bear in mind that these people have no concept of free speech."

In short, when native-born Americans had prevented an Arab American from continuing to express his views, Americans blamed it on Arab culture and its supposed lack of basic human rights. Yet I think that if I had asked any of those Americans if they themselves believed in freedom of expression, they would have said they did. Being an American really is a complex fate, I think, in that the lip service we so often give to our high ideals has to be accompanied by careful and constant self-examination. The fate is made more complex by the power that many Americans have throughout the world, which can be used to prevent others from asking Americans the kinds of questions that make us reflect on our beliefs.

The fact that America has freedom of expression does not necessarily mean that Americans are exposed to a range of opinion. As I remember the first amendment, it only says that the government cannot prohibit freedom of speech. It doesn't say that an employer can't ask a newspaper editor to stop publishing certain kinds of articles, or that the editor can't comply. For that matter, it doesn't say that an employer can't fire an employee for writing articles his superiors disagree with. The same thing that happened to Hani in Sharjah could happen in the United States. Americans have a greater degree of freedom of expression than people in other countries where I have lived, such as China and Egypt and Saudi Arabia. But the degree is still limited by what the majority is willing to tolerate, and by what will sell newspapers. A democratic government in itself can't establish an ideal degree of freedom of expression if the majority of people don't want certain kinds of issues discussed, or don't want the ideas of certain groups of people to become public. Living in the United States, it can be hard to realize the extent to which real freedom of expression is in danger, because we don't know what to look for. It's hard to know what's missing.

At the same time that the university was embroiled in its furor over Hani's articles, I myself had published an article in the *Progressive* criticizing the bombings as well, and I think the difference between the response to my article and that to Hani's is illustrative. First, no one at the university asked me to stop writing. In fact, both the dean and the chancellor wrote me polite notes congratulating me on the publication. Part of the reason for the difference in response, of course, was where I had printed my article. The faculty members who were disturbed at seeing American policy criticized were unlikely to read the *Progressive.*

But I think there was another reason why the university

responded differently to my article, and why no one objected. I think it also helped that I am not an Arab American, in part because this made what I said more likely to be taken as honest and well-intentioned criticism. It seems ironic that knowing less about the Middle East should make me more credible, and that having being born in a country rather than deliberately choosing it should make my loyalties less questionable, but I don't think I am merely being cynical in feeling that this is true. Arab Americans publish scholarly books about the Middle East for a few hundred fellow scholars to read, but I have seldom seen Arab names in the mainstream press. And when I have collaborated with Arab Americans on opinion articles, editors have asked me if I could resubmit the pieces under my name alone. They did not do this because they themselves were prejudiced against Arabs; if this were the case, they wouldn't have been willing to publish a pro-Arab article such as mine in the first place. They were considering whether their readers would find the story believable, and they were considering the demands of the marketplace.

This reluctance to print the views of Arab Americans might also apply to other ethnic groups, because when I thought about it, I realized that most of the columnists and news commentators who help to shape public opinion are Americans of European ancestry. True, African American, Asian American, and Hispanic American announcers read the news or host morning talk shows, poets and fiction writers convey the experience of being a "hyphenated American" to the relatively small group of Americans who read literature, and African Americans have a strong influence on popular music. However, few minority thinkers have the opportunity to express their political opinions in the mass media, particularly if their ideas might be critical of American society or policies. "Pushing the envelope" means pushing the limits of taste, not expressing challenging and carefully thought-out opinions. Although America is made up of peoples who originally came from different cultures and whose values and political ideas were shaped by different cultural experiences, it sometimes seems that minorities can speak to their fellow Americans only if they agree not to challenge conventional thinking. If this is true of foreign-born and non-European Americans, it is even more true of non-Americans who might have valuable perspectives on American society and culture.

Americans are in a different situation from many other educated people in that it is harder to find intelligently written articles that challenge the morality of American foreign policy in the mainstream American press. Those few newspapers and magazines that are critical (the *Progressive,* for example) are often not available outside large cities. In smaller, less powerful countries, the local press has to compete with the foreign press and international mass media. Even if some local people in these countries would rather not have certain kinds of problems discussed and would prefer not to hear what foreigners say about them, they are nevertheless exposed to these ideas on international radio and television. The American media doesn't have to compete with a foreign media within its own borders. This situation creates a lack of competition in the marketplace of ideas. (When American media does have to compete with foreign media, the types of coverage, the range of opinion, and the ethnicity of the reporters change dramatically. I saw this for myself when I noted the difference between the international versions of *Time* and *Newsweek* and their domestic editions, and between CNN International and domestic CNN.) The lack of exposure to controversial ideas makes Americans more likely to be shocked by such ideas when they do encounter them, and perhaps more tempted to view such ideas as dangerous.

I think that this lack of exposure to different values and ideas, however, has a worse effect than simply making Americans intolerant of such opinions. When native-born white Americans do not hear the voices of the non-white and foreign-born, the voiceless people can come to seem less valuable as human beings. When one loses his voice, he loses part of his humanity, and thus any injustice that befalls him comes to seem less important. Ten years earlier, I had seen, I think, an example of just how dangerous such assumptions are, when five Asian students were killed in the university town where I was teaching and no one ever learned who killed them or why.

A Window into Equal Justice

I suppose I remembered that terrible event because in Sharjah, I myself was a foreigner again, and I was living among other foreigners. This made me relive what it is like to live in a culture and country that is not one's own, where one doesn't know what to expect, where one feels like an outsider. That year in Sharjah, many of the Americans at the university feared that they might become the targets of a terrorist attack, particularly during Ramadan, because that was when the World Trade Center in New York had been bombed in 1993. In fact, when the American embassy issued a warning to all Americans advising us to keep a low profile, several faculty members refused to display university parking stickers, fearing that being identified with an American university might provoke attacks against them. So many faculty complained about the lack of security at the gates that the Sharjah government finally posted armed guards to check the identification of everyone entering the campus. Americans felt under siege. I don't think we were ever in real danger, yet the fear was contagious. And then I reflected on what it would be like to live as a foreigner in America, and I remembered the five students who had been burned to death at Southern Illinois University in Carbondale, Illinois.

Carbondale itself is a small town of about twenty thousand, dwarfed by the university, surrounded by farming and mining country, and so pretty and friendly that few people would suspect the racial tensions that lie beneath its surface. Culturally, it is both a part of the Midwest and part of the South. Most of the local farmers are white, although these farmers employ large numbers of Hispanic migrant workers. The town does have a small African American community, but these African Americans seldom go into the "white" sections of town around the university or into the surrounding countryside. I remember African American students repeatedly writing about being told that their patronage was not welcome at local restaurants and bars. In addition to this fairly sizable African American student body at the university, there were several thousand international students, many of them Asian. The racial tension among whites, blacks, and Hispanics was intense enough that the English department had severe problems recruiting and retaining Hispanic and African American professors. I really didn't know very much about the problems the Asian students faced until the Pyramids Apartment House was burned.

About what actually happened, I know only what I read and saw in news reports, which was surprisingly little considering the gravity of the crime. But I did know how the people around me responded to it, or rather, how they failed to respond to it. I first heard about the fire when I suddenly heard Carbondale mentioned in the CBS evening news. There had been a fire at an apartment building housing Asian students, the report said, leaving four students dead and another critically injured. (That student, an Indonesian girl, died of her burns a few days later.) That was the first and the last time any report of the fire or the deaths of the students appeared on the national news. The next day, the school paper carried a front-page picture of ATF agents sifting through the smoldering remains of the building and the announcement that the ATF had determined arson as the cause. The fire had been set in the middle of the night, when most of the students were asleep, and whoever had started it had poured gasoline in the stairwells, making escape impossible for people on the upper floors of the three-story building. Whoever set the fire had wanted to kill people.

The local police chief immediately stated that he believed that the fire was a deliberate homicide. But he also said that he did not think it was a hate crime. He had interviewed survivors, he said, and none of them reported being threatened or harassed. All of the Americans I spoke to took up this refrain; nice, ordinary Americans about whom there was seemingly nothing “not to like”: my favorite students, the good-natured department secretary, my friends in the English department. Carbondale did not have hate crimes. Hate crimes occurred in countries like Germany. There had to be some other reason for the arson.

I myself didn't understand why the police didn't consider racial hatred as a possible motive for the crime. How could they rule out a motive if they didn't know who set the fire? It seemed to me that the fact that the Asian students said they hadn't been threatened didn't mean that they hadn't been the targets of a hate crime. In the first place, the arsonist could have set the fire with the intention of killing Asians without making any threats first. Or the Asian students might have been afraid to tell the American police if they had been threatened. I had heard American students complain in general about the Asians students, saying that they tied up the computer labs, ruined the curve in math classes, and did not belong in the United States. I can remember pointing out to a boy in class that the foreign students paid twice the tuition that Illinois students did and were going to go back to their own countries when they finished college, and having him reply that they shouldn't be allowed into the country anyway.

Moreover, although everyone said that there must be some other motive for the crime, I never heard any other plausible theories. The five students who died all seemed to be quiet, studious young men and women, not the sort to provoke murderous hatred. And what sort of personal grudge would make someone want to kill five unrelated people of different nationalities who had nothing in common except their race? The victims were not even all foreign, since one young man was a Chinese American. I heard rumors from American students that the five people killed were not the intended targets, and that the arsonist was someone who had been cheated on a drug deal by an Asian student who was never identified. The five students who were killed, they implied, were simply collateral damage. No one, however, seemed to have any evidence to support this theory, and indeed no police official ever suggested in print that this was a possible motive for the killing.

I can't say that either the local people or the American students and faculty behaved badly. Two local churches immediately began to find temporary shelters and new apartments for the students who had lost their homes and to collect clothing, books, and money to help the survivors replace what they had lost in the fire. The International Students Club on campus collected donations to cover the medical expenses of the surviving students, and American faculty and students contributed very generously. I was in the student union when an American boy signed over a check for two hundred dollars, his work-study paycheck for the week, which made me feel rather cheap about the twenty dollars I had just contributed. And yet, everyone seemed to want to treat the fire and the deaths as a terrible tragedy, not a terrible crime.

I suppose I might have reacted in the same way if I hadn't taught for a year in China and lived in Japan. I could at least begin to understand what this crime had done not just to the victims, but to their families. I could imagine all the hope and pride the parents must have felt when their children were accepted at an American university. They could have sent their children to a university at home, but they thought an American university would make their son or daughter a real citizen of the world. Most of these Asian students didn't have rich parents. They had parents who saved their whole lives to send them to America. And now all that hope was dead, all the sacrifice was for nothing, and what those parents had done out of love had ended up killing the children they loved so much.

The criminal investigation that followed received no coverage in the national press and little coverage in the local press. The crime was never solved. No one was ever arrested. No one was ever even named as an official suspect. The *Southern Illinoisan,* the regional newspaper, hardly mentioned the investigation, and the nearest big city newspaper, the *St. Louis Post Dispatch,* carried just a few small reports in its back pages. Only the student newspaper continued to interview the police about the investigation, or to talk to the students' parents about their concerns.

The parents had come all the way from Japan and Taiwan to attend the memorial services; they had been saving, they told the student reporters, to come for their children's graduations, and never expected to be coming to their funerals instead. I remember one Japanese man was quoted as saying that he would not go home until he found out who had killed his daughter and why, and that he hoped that the state attorney's office would seek the death penalty for the arsonist. Nevertheless, he must have finally gone home without this knowledge, because the investigation led nowhere, nothing happened, and the rest of the students and faculty and townspeople went on with their ordinary lives. It wasn't precisely that no one cared; it was simply that they did not consider it to be their problem.

A few months after the fire that killed the five students, the World Trade Center in New York was attacked, and the suspects arrested shortly afterward. My elderly downstairs neighbor greeted me one morning with the news, "They've caught the people who bombed the Trade Center. Isn't that wonderful!" I remember at the time noting that exactly the same number of people were killed, and yet one crime was solved almost immediately among daily national and international news coverage, while the other was never solved. I figured that the main reason for this difference is that one crime happened in New York, where the building damaged was a prominent public landmark, whereas the other crime happened in a small town and the building was just an ordinary apartment building for students. The local Carbondale police certainly didn't have the resources of the New York City police and the FBI, arson cases were notoriously difficult to solve, and the police really couldn't be blamed for failing to find the arsonist.

And then I noticed that when American students were killed in various accidents—a school bus wreck in Kentucky, a bonfire collapse in Texas—the events received national coverage for several days, the students' pictures appeared on TV screens, and the victims' families were interviewed on the morning talk shows. The accidents—and they were accidents in these cases, not crimes—were thoroughly investigated. It seemed as if the deaths of American young people mattered, and the deaths of Asian students studying in our country did not matter to nearly the same degree. It was possible for Americans to feel this way, I think, because they hadn't seen and couldn't imagine the families that had raised these young men and women. They couldn't understand who these students and their families were within their own societies, or what they might have had to contribute both to their own societies and to the world. They hadn't heard the voices of

Asian Americans, much less the voices of Chinese, Japanese, or Indonesians.

I don't think anyone would have said that the deaths of the Asians didn't matter as much as if they had all been white Americans, and perhaps no one even realized that he or she felt that way. Most of the people I knew would have been courteous to foreign students they encountered and would have been offended if anyone suggested that they had any prejudice toward foreigners. The distinction between how Americans viewed Americans and how they viewed foreigners was so subtle that it would have been imperceptible to anyone who didn't stop to consider how the press and the townspeople and the law would have reacted if the students had all been Americans, and of European ancestry. As it was, the white Americans in Carbondale were shocked and saddened by the fire and the deaths, but very few were angry or felt deeply concerned that whoever killed the students should be tried for his crime.

Back in Sharjah, when we were all sitting around waiting for terrorists to bomb the university, I wondered how it must have felt to be an Asian student in Carbondale. If someone really attacked AUS, it would have been an international incident. We at least had the dubious assurance that a terrorist attack would make the news and that our government would insist on an investigation. I couldn't help wondering why it should be considered terrorism if Americans were attacked by foreigners, but if foreigners were attacked in America, it was simply an unpleasant incident that was best forgotten. How must it have felt to those Asian students who lived in Carbondale after the fire, knowing that they could be killed, that whoever killed them could go free, and that none of the bland, smiling American faces around them would view it as anything out of the ordinary?

Looking at America from Sharjah and remembering those events, I saw a different America than I would have seen if I had stayed at home. I began to have a sense of some of the unspoken and usually unquestioned assumptions that defined the American character and that came out of the unique combination of America's great wealth and political power, its isolation from other cultures, and its ability to silence other voices. These assumptions are so pervasive that we often don't even know that we believe them; they are the element in which we live. The fate of being an American is that we define our characters by our responses to those assumptions.

PART FOUR Off the Beaten Track

Savages, we call them, because their manners differ from ours, which we imagine to be the height of civility; they think the same of theirs.

—Benjamin Franklin, "Remarks Concerning the Savages of North America"

Teaching Multiculturally and Being Multicultural

Teaching Multiculturally

The English department, composed mostly of Americans of various origins, was looking for a multicultural essay collection that could serve as a reader for our composition course, and we found dozens of them in American publishers' catalogs. The problem was that we couldn't use any of them to teach students who were not Americans and had no particular wish to become Americans. Our students had come to us because they wanted an American-style education added to their identities as Emiratis or Palestinians or Indians or whatever they were to begin with. In fact, most of our students had some familiarity with more than one culture already. In many cases, while their parents had come from other countries, the students themselves had been raised in the Emirates and had seen their "native" counties only on visits with their grandparents. They all had been exposed to American popular culture, and they all spoke a second language. It seemed to me that in many ways our students were multicultural, but not in the sense in which that word is usually used in the United States.

I began to think, then, of how multiculturalism should be taught, and of what it meant to be multicultural.

Given America's political and cultural influence over societies that many Americans have never even heard of, Americans need the kinds of perspectives that multicultural studies can provide. Multicultural perspectives might have made the people of Carbondale more disturbed that the killer of five people never faced justice, and my colleagues at AUS less disturbed that an Arab American held different political opinions from theirs. Unfortunately, many texts that are called multicultural may not actually be multicultural at all, any more than new improved brands of detergent are really new and improved.

Not only freshman composition, but literature, history, and probably all the humanities can be taught from a multicultural perspective. This approach begins with making students aware of the existence of other cultures, but it can't stop there. Most American students are already aware of the existence of other cultures, even though they may not have ever met a foreigner or an American from a different ethnic group. What the American college students I have encountered usually do not know is the strengths and weaknesses of these other cultures and how these strengths and weaknesses are interwoven. Often, they are also unaware that they can learn not only about other cultures, but from them. These are concepts that multicultural approaches to writing and literature could teach but seldom do.

The multicultural readers we examined all seemed to be designed to show monocultural American students that their fellow Americans whose ancestors—or parents—had come from different continents were really just as American as they were. These essays told the stories of articulate African Americans who managed to win respect from the white people who had once looked down upon them; they told about American born Asian Americans' struggles against the stifling conventions of their parents' culture; they described Hispanic students' struggles to learn English and their ambivalent feelings about their Spanish-speaking parents. The "multicultural" readers seemed aimed at the admirable goal of reducing racial and ethnic prejudice within the United States, but they often failed to show that not everyone wants to become American at the price of giving up the values or the perspectives of her ancestral culture. They didn't include the voices of first- and second-generation Americans who wanted to include America within themselves without forgetting the knowledge and experiences that shaped them and their parents. They didn't include essays that suggested there are valid ways of defining oneself and behaving toward others that differed from those most American students knew. Adding a few essays by minority writers to the standard texts is not enough in itself to make an anthology multicultural, if the ideas in the essays simply echo contemporary received opinion.

What applies to the multicultural readers also applies to many of the multicultural literature courses in American universities. In these introductory literature courses, American students often first encounter literature by writers who are neither British nor American. Such courses, called "Literature of the Modern World" or even "Introduction to Literature," are usually electives open to first year English majors and to nonmajors who need to fill a humanities requirement. The courses include works by European, African, Asian, and South American writers, all of whom come from cultures very different from one another and about which the instructor herself often knows relatively little. After all, undergraduate and graduate programs in English normally don't require courses in the political and cultural history of Asia, Africa, or South America, or even a very detailed study of European history. The instructor must either learn a great deal of world history, anthropology, and political science at once, or present the literature as isolated artifacts. If the teachers themselves are unfamiliar with the context of the works, both student and teacher have only the text in front of them to tell them what another culture believes and values. The text is not enough.

For one thing, it is necessarily to know the society which shaped a writer and to which a writer is responding. I think it is a mistake to view literature as representative of a society, as I found out from trying to read al-Murr before I had come to the UAE. And yet, it is a great temptation to do this if a literary work is the only source of information at hand about that culture. Reading an Egyptian novel, for instance, doesn't necessarily show an American reader how Egyptians think and feel. It shows how one Egyptian views the world around him. Societies don't write stories and poems. Writers do. Each writer has a vision of the world that comes out of his own experience. His consciousness, his voice, has shaped that view into words, which are sometimes very different than the English words that the students read on the page. The writers shape their work out of their own pain, pain over the problems of their countries, and pain over their own condition as thinking people within that country. Many Asian and African writers are Western-educated men and women who are consciously writing to a Western audience, not to their own people. Some of the writers are torn in two by the disparity between the culture in which they were raised and the culture of their education. But without being able to see the background to which the writer is responding, one's view of the text in the foreground is so distorted that the shape is sometimes barely recognizable.

The case of the work of "hyphenated Americans," such as American-born Asian and Hispanic writers, is equally problematic if the instructor teaches the work as representative of the values of a minority subculture or worse, as a way of understanding a foreign culture. The writers with foreign-born parents are often trying as Americans to understand the world their parents left and why their parents left it. The fact that their parents or grandparents did choose to leave the old country in itself gives these writers a very different perspective on that society than that of those who stayed.

"These Chinese Americans are very old fashioned," one of my Chinese students once told me after reading Maxine Hong Kingston and Amy Tan. "In China today, we call these attitudes 'feudal thinking.' " She was referring, I think, not to the writers, who seemed completely American to her, but to the attitudes of the protagonists' "Chinese" parents. The China of Tan and Kingston was a different China than the country my Chinese student lived in, but it was the only China my American students would learn of in that course.

The combinations of the works selected by the anthologies and the ways in which American instructors present the work usually does not present non-Western values and ideas in a particularly favorable light. The result is that American students end up saying, as one of my students in Southern Illinois said of Amy Tan's *The Joy Luck Club,* "Those girls sure were lucky that they were born in American and not back in China like their mothers." Or they say, as another student did to a colleague of mine about Achebe's *Things Fall Apart*, "Yeah, Yeah, I get the picture. People are all the same underneath. People aren't animals, even if they live in a jungle. So why do I have to read this whole dull book to find this out?" In fact, that student's response was more broadminded than many. My own students had been so horrified that the precolonial West Africans killed twin babies that they were unable to see any redeeming virtues in any of the characters.

There is something within people in many societies, I think, that finds satisfaction in saying, "See how awful those people are. Thank God we're not like that." Some students even seem to fear that it is vaguely unpatriotic to see too much value in the literature of another society. I had to struggle against these assumptions when I taught American literature to students in China and Egypt. In American multicultural literature courses, the combination of the texts selected and the instructors' lack of knowledge can confirm this ethnocentric response.

Perhaps this attitude would change if more anthology editors were multicultural themselves and could provide a framework for understanding the texts of another culture, and if they included caveats about generalizing about the culture from the text. As it is, the editors often seem to know little more about the literature than the students. (I remember one textbook that contained a footnote to explain a reference in a short story by the Egyptian writer Yusef Idrees. The note identified two popular Egyptian singers of the 1960s, Abdel-Wahib and Umm Kalsoum, as the religious figures after which they were named, which is rather like saying Peter, Paul, and Mary were early saints of the Christian church.)

If it is too much to expect editors to be familiar with so many diverse literatures in detail, and I am not sure that it is, they still have other alternatives. It would certainly help if a literary scholar from the country in which the literature was written provided an introduction to each work. If a Nigerian scholar wrote an introduction to Achebe, or an Egyptian scholar to Mahfouz, the works would be infinitely easier for both American teachers and students to understand. The teachers themselves could invite international students and foreign-born professors to sit in on classes in which their country's literature was being discussed and add their insights. The problem is that teachers and editors alike seem to be unused to thinking of foreigners or foreign-born Americans as people who can add to their knowledge—exactly the problem that the courses are supposed to remedy.

Being Multicultural

Many years ago, when I was teaching in Saudi Arabia, I was talking to my office partner, Rana, a Saudi woman whose grandparents had come from Palestine, about her decision not to stay in the United States when she had finished graduate school in Ohio. Her two daughters had been born in the United States and were thus American citizens. Under American law at that time, this would have enabled her and her husband to stay in the United States and apply for American citizenship. Her husband, a Palestinian with Jordanian travel documents, had wanted to stay in the United States, declaring that Americans treated Palestinians no worse than his fellow Arabs did. Rana was a well-educated and broadminded woman who often found the conservatism of Saudi Arabia stifling and hypocritical. And yet, she did not want to stay in the United States.

"I want my daughters to grow up to be polite women who know who they are and respect themselves," she told me, "and I don't think it would be easy for them to do that in America."

I thought I understood what she meant, and I could understand why she had made the choice to stay in Saudi Arabia. The educated middle-class Arabs I knew seem to put more emphasis on formal manners and encourage children and teenagers to interact with adults of all ages, which gives young Arab men and women a kind of social poise that their American counterparts often lack. It might well be difficult for an Arab American child to retain her self-respect and a respect for her heritage when Arabs were so constantly misrepresented and vilified in the American media, and it would be equally difficult to acquire the sense of self-respect that, for many Arab women, seemed to come from conforming to their society's standards of sexual propriety. They would probably never learn to read and write Arabic, so that much of their literary heritage would be lost to them. I could certainly understand why a mother would rather have her daughters grow up monocultural than subject them to the difficulties of growing up as bicultural Arab Americans. And yet, they could have gained from American culture as well.

I think that part of the reason that Rana made her decision was because she wasn't bicultural herself. She spoke fluent English, had a master's degree from an American university, and had lived in the United States for three years, but I suspect that she had only seen enough of America to see some of what was wrong with it, not what it could give her daughters: the intellectual stimulation, the self-reliance, the opportunities for accomplishment. She had lived in the United States during the late 1980s when the media was filled with lurid stories about children being abused in day-care centers, and when pictures of missing children were on every milk carton. Several of the young American mothers whom Rana knew home-schooled their children, claiming that drugs were rampant in public schools and this was the only way to keep their children safe. Rana had no way of knowing that these women, and their opinions, did not represent the majority. She never had the chance to experience the quiet beauty of the Ohio countryside, nor enjoy the museums and symphonies of its big cities, nor to meet thoughtful and intelligent Americans who had found their places within American society, nor to see American children who were doing well in American public schools. In part, Rana missed this side of America because she was afraid that her children would be kidnapped by drug-crazed child molesters if she let them out of her sight. Who could blame her? And after all, Rana and her husband were in the country to get their degrees, not to make an intensive study of American culture and society. Nevertheless, she saw, in effect, what confirmed her opinions about the superiority of her own culture, just as my American students saw in foreign literature only what confirmed their own beliefs.

This made me reflect again on what it means to be multicultural, and how people become multicultural. Being multicultural is more than knowing another society's arts, customs, and manners. After all, many of the people within a culture are unfamiliar with its high art, and in the cultures in which I have lived, people have been very willing to overlook an outsider's social gaffes. Culture, and being multicultural, is something much deeper than this. Culture is comprised of so many things—the ideas a society discusses publically, the virtues it tends to value over others, the ways in which it responds to people within the society who question its assumptions. It is the backdrop against which each person within the society defines himself.

Multiculturalism demands a great tolerance for contradiction and ambiguity and a great capacity for empathy, as the background behind the self shifts like a turning kaleidoscope. One society might place a high value on being assertive, and another on enduring hardship without complaint. And every society has its own contradictory values, as when Americans value both individualism and "being a team player." Being multicultural means being aware of the complexity of these backgrounds and being willing to imagine, at least, the ways in which a person can define herself against the often conflicting ideas and values and assumptions that make up another culture.

It is much easier to be monocultural than to try to sort through conflicting sets of beliefs that often each have their own inadequacies. Confronted with the difficulties of living with differing sets of beliefs, it is easier to become homocultural (associating only with people in ones own culture) or schizocultural (compartmentalizing the differing cultures so that one doesn't even see the contradictions between them) than to be multicultural. When encountering another culture, we find that it is easiest to retreat into generalizations and stereotypes. Retreat. Constriction. Contraction. Multiculturalism is the opposite. It says, "I think I know who I am. I know I don't know who you are. I know something about the society that shaped you, but I don't know how you have responded to it until you tell me. I am willing to let knowing who you are change who I am."

Dune Planet at the Millennium

It avails not, time nor place—distance avails not

—Walt Whitman,
"Crossing Brooklyn Ferry"

I was living in three different places at once. I was living within myself somewhere outside the United States, looking in at my own society with a vision made clearer by distance. I was living within a landscape whose rough beauty and unexpected lushness dazzled me, among people whom I had come to like and trust. And I was living in the heart of an alien place, in the midst of a history and geography that were not my own, surrounded by people who had grown up in a different culture. How much did place matter in making me who I was, I often wondered, and how much of where I was now would become part of me?

To me, the countryside of northwestern Pennsylvania, where I lived the first half of my life, seemed the landscape of my heart, with its dusty country roads winding through fields of wild mustard and chickory. Its gray, cool summers and its lake-effect snowstorms in winter are a part of my inner weather. What did it mean, then, to be in a place so very different?

I thought of this in particular the night the millennium changed, as I lay on a sand dune looking up at the same stars I had watched almost a half century earlier from the front lawn of my parents' house. The sand under me was just slightly cool. A hundred yards away was the encampment where my friends and I were staying for the night, a tour guide's cleaned up and modernized version of a bedouin camp. It was rather like camping in a state park in the United States, except that silhouetted on the crest of a nearby dune was a line of tethered camels, patiently chewing their cuds and waiting for the young mothers in the camp below to bring their children for the promised camel rides. Except for the stars and the flickering campfires that the tour guides had started in big open hearths to ward off the evening chill, it was dark; and except for an occasional muffled laugh drifting up from the camp, all was silent.

I had agreed to come on this trip partly because I had not yet really experienced the desert. I had only looked at it from the window of a car or taken short walks in the open spaces outside the university gate. But I had also come because my friend Amal had called me up and wanted to know what I was doing on New Year's Eve.

"Nothing," I said. "Maybe grading papers."

"Then come with us to the desert. We're going dune bashing. Then we'll stay overnight in the desert. There'll be Arabic music and dancing and food. A whole group of us from the college are going. You ought to come."

"I don't want to go dune bashing," I said. "I'm afraid of heights and speed. The other women all have children who will run around shrieking like wild things until they are exhausted, and then they will whine and cling to their mothers and no one will be able to carry on an adult conversation. I don't want to sleep on the ground because my muscles will get so stiff I won't be able to walk the next day. I'm an old lady."

"You don't have to go dune bashing," she countered. "You can have an adult conversation with me. They have promised us cots and sleeping bags. And do you want to be an old lady who sits at home and marks papers on New Year's Eve or old lady who follows in the footsteps of Lawrence and Thesinger?"

So I went.

There were ten of us piled into two land rovers: Anita, a Lebanese American woman from my department, her husband, and their three children; Mona, a woman who taught in the Arabic department and her two boys; Amal; and me. At about eighty miles an hour, we set out across the desert highway that spans the peninsula, and the scrub and gravel plain flew by in a blur.

After about two hours, the driver pulled off into the sand and slowed slightly. The sand slithered under tire as we bounced up dunes and flew around S-shaped curves. I held on to the handgrip over the window with both hands and said, "Holy shit!"

"Whee! We're dune bashing! Faster!" one of the little boys yelled.

"No, honey, we're not dune bashing yet. We've got to drop Dr. Caesar off at the camp first," Mona explained.

"Could you drive more slowly," I pleaded.

"I want to go fast," the little boy insisted, and then turned to me. "What did you come here for anyway if you don't want to go fast?"

"Honey, that's not nice," Mona chided.

"That's ok," I said, between clenched teeth. "I was just asking myself the same question."

And then we were at the camp, a series of tents down in a valley among the dunes, arranged in square around a raised platform.

"Consider this camp your camp," the guide informed me."Walk wherever you want. Make yourself at home. But don't lose yourself!"

Good advice. I hopped out of the land rover and looked around, stunned into silence by the silence around me. The dunes were not just beige sand, as I had thought. There were sprinklings of a dark red brown as well, and in other places the sand was almost white. The top of each dune formed a sharp crest, like a wave frozen in motion. I clambered up the nearest dune, my feet sinking into the loose sand at every step, and then looked at the view. There was nothing but dune after dune and the faint plume of dust from the disappearing land rover. One side of the dune was packed firm, with little ripples like the ones at the bottom of shallow water along a beach. What were the physics of dunes, I wondered, that caused them to make these patterns? The wind blew a mist of sand over the crest, like snow blowing from a drift in a blizzard. In fact, walking in the loose sand was like walking in dry snow, except in the snow, I would have sunk all the way to the ground without snowshoes—and here, this was the ground. Why didn't a person sink in sand the way one did in snow? I tramped around the perimeter of the campsite, thinking about all of this and listening to the silence. Here, there was not even a birdsong.

Of course, real bedouins wouldn't be camping out in the dunes, I reminded myself. There was no grazing here. The bedouins would have been back on the scrub and gravel plain, where camels and goats could graze on Sodom's apple and ghuff trees, and where the thorn trees provided shelter from the sun. This would have been just a treacherous space to traverse on the way to the market towns in the mountains. I wondered if anything lived here. Off in the distance, I could see a hawk circling, so there must be something. Somewhere, there must be something that could be eaten. Perhaps there were a few snakes and jerboa, the little rodents that looked like puff balls on legs. Even among the dunes, then, there must be a few little wadis where a bit of vegetation could survive. And yet, it seemed to be a world of sand, a world in which nothing living could eat or drink. Whatever life there was must be beneath the surface of things, hidden out of the sight of people like me, who didn't know what to look for. Yet once, this place had been full of life. The fossils in the rocks just a few dozen miles away testified to that. First, it had been ocean. And then it had been grassland. Human civilization had arisen and flourished for millennia here, from the ancient kingdoms of Dilmun and Magan to the great medieval caliphates.

I thought about Frank Herbert's novel *Dune,* which Leona's son Adam had lent me a few months earlier. In the dune planet of the novel, native people called Fremen, who sounded very much like Arabs and lived in mountain caves (like the Jebali of Oman), plotted ways to free their planet from an alien empire and to transform their planet's ecology into a world of green again. Sitting here now on the dune, looking out at nothing but dunes in all directions, it wasn't hard to imagine a dune planet. And it wasn't hard to imagine that I was its only inhabitant.

I could entertain this idea with composure because now, in the camp below, I could see Indian workmen moving around, setting up tables and charcoal grills and unloading boxes of food. Because it was Ramadan, I guessed, we would eat as soon as the sun went down, which meant that the others would be back in about half an hour. In fact, in the distance I could see a cloud of dust, which was probably the land rovers returning. My world of barrenness and solitude was real but temporary. I could only begin to imagine what life must have been for people to whom this landscape and the less picturesque plains of stunted trees were not just scenery, but home. Hunger and thirst and dust must have been constants, or always in wait, just as snow and cold had been for me during the long hard winters I'd known as a girl. This was a glimpse of that life of the past, I thought, without any of its real discomforts.

I did, however, get an experience of hunger and discomfort that was far more intense that I had anticipated, but this was due to the tour company's poor organizational skills, not to their impulse to share with us the privations of the desert. When my friends returned, we were invited to sit in the brightly colored striped tents, where low tables awaited food. Alongside the table were cushionlike objects for us to sit on. They were not cushions, because cushions are by definition stuffed with something soft, like foam or feathers, and these objects felt as if they were probably stuffed with sand. The only difference between them and any other sandbags was that they had lacy little covers. Mona, the Arabic teacher who had been fasting all day, asked if the sun was down yet, and hearing that it was, took a drink of water from her thermos and lit a cigarette.

"Now where's the food?" she said crossly.

"I'll ask," Amal said, and went off to try to locate one of the tour guides.

I watched the stars come out, one by one, as the light faded, while the one man in our group, who taught astronomy, pointed out that the bright star just coming up over the horizon was Jupiter. The fainter light just to the left of it was Mars, which I could see through my binoculars as a glimmer of red. This landscape could have been the landscape of Mars, with its reflection looking back at me over millions of miles and millions of years. Perhaps Mars was a version of what earth might become thousands of years from now.

Amal came back and sat down, looking like a person who did not have good news. "Nine thirty," she announced. "They are waiting for all the tour groups who have come from Dubai and Abu Dhabi. But in the meantime, we can ride camels and have our hands painted with henna. And they are serving Arabic coffee and dates."

To me, this seemed like a very poor substitute for real food.

Over the loudspeaker, someone was tuning an oud. The young mothers gathered their children to climb up to the dunes above the camp so that they could ride the camels before it got too dark to see. Then a man began a soft, meditative song with a haunting and wandering melody.

"It's classical Arabic," Amal told me when I asked about it. "I don't think I could do it justice if I tried to translate. It's a love song."

By the time he stopped, it was completely dark.

"Let's go ride the camels," Amal suggested. But I wasn't about to get on an animal whose back was so far from the ground, especially an animal that got up rump first, and then be led around sand dunes in the dark.

"That's how the camel caravans used to travel," Amal pointed out to me, "so this really would give you a sense of what the old days were like."

"Because it was too hot to travel in the daytime?" I asked. "But how did they find their way?"

"By the stars," she said. Of course. It made perfect sense. How else could you find your way through a shifting ocean of sand? I wondered then if celestial navigation had begun in the desert, where the stars were always visible, rather than as a way for sailors to find their course at sea.

On my way out of the camp, I passed by the tent of some Germans, who were drinking beer they'd had the foresight to bring with them, and another tent full of people who were dancing a Lebanese debkah to the music of a portable cassette recorder. Since the debkah involves a great deal of leaping and stamping, it was also a good way to ward off the evening chill, which was just beginning to settle

Up on the dune, I trained my binoculars on the stars. Already, I could see more stars than I had in years. There was Orion, and just above him, the Pleiades. I had lived far too long under city lights that obscured the stars, and the stars I saw now were the stars I remembered.

As soon as I was up on the dune, all the noise of the camp disappeared. There was nothing but the tinkle of the bells on the camels as the guides led them up and down the dunes and back again. I watched the riders through the binoculars and saw that Amal was as good as her word. She was on a camel. I also heard her screech when her camel suddenly flopped to its knees, almost pitching her over its head.

In four hours, it would be another century. In four hours, it would be another millennium. I was so hungry I wanted to kill one of those camels and eat the whole thing raw, and yet above me arched an eternity of light, millions of miles away, light years away, light millennia away. If anyone from one of those planets orbiting one of those far away stars landed here now, what would they make of what they saw? When I looked up at the stars, I easily imagined a *Star Trek* world, a *Dune* planet world. If space travelers came here now, they'd find a group of people speaking half a dozen different languages, they'd see electric generators and a water storage tank to give us lights and flush toilets, they'd see four-wheel-drive vehicles almost the size of tanks—and they'd see camels and bonfires and tents and sand, blowing and drifting dunes of sand that stretched for miles and miles in all directions. To what place, to what century, would they think they had come?

I saw a slight figure climbing the side of the dune, and soon Amal was sitting beside me.

"You've found a good place," she observed. "Above, you can see the stars, and below, you can see if they are making any moves toward bringing any food out." She pulled her shawl closer around her.

"I guess we'll all get warm again when the dancing starts," I suggested.

"I don't think there is going to be any dancing," Amal said, "because of Ramadan."

"I hear you're an antidancing person anyway," I said, and Amal laughed.

"So you've heard that story," she said. "Let me tell you what really happened."

And what really happened was almost as interesting as the preparations for food going on below. When Amal had been a graduate student in the United States and active in the Arab Students Union, the university she was attending had sponsored an international day. The Arab students were told they should set up a tent and hire a belly dancer, all with money from the student activities fund. At first, most of the Arab students hadn't raised any objection. After all, they said, it wasn't their own money, and besides, a belly dancer might be fun. But Amal had pointed out that money from the student activities fund was their money as much as anybody else's, and that the Americans were reducing a fifteen-hundred-year-old civilization to a hootchy-kootchy dance.

"Did they ask the African American students to play banjos, tap dance, and serve watermelon? No!" She said emphatically. And she had eventually persuaded both the Arab student group and the student activities coordinator to accept her point of view. Instead of having the tent and the belly dancer, the Arab students had played some traditional North African and Levantine music to a backdrop of slides of Middle Eastern art, and some of the Palestinian and Lebanese men had danced a debkah.

Graduate school often seemed a world away now. It seemed ironic that the promotion of the tent and belly dance as the epitome of Arab culture, the stereotype that she had fought so hard against twenty-five years earlier, was now exactly what we were experiencing tonight for ourselves. I also wondered if the Palestinians were any better off than they had been twenty-five years earlier, despite the political plays and the endless promises. I looked at Amal's sharp profile and tried to imagine that young graduate student, and then I realized she was still there, as the girl I had been was still within me. We can travel back to these mental places because they are seldom wholly gone. Other memories build up over them and change the outward shapes of our personalities, but somewhere, who we were when we were young remains buried within us like lost cities. And yet, the shapes that had built up around these two middle-aged women made them more similar than the two young women had been, so that now, covered by the layers of the places where we had lived, Amal and I were not so very different from each other.

To pass the time while we were waiting for dinner, Amal told me more stories about her life, about her research into child labor practices all over the world and what she had learned about them. This topic was a long way away from her academic field, but it made as much sense as my straying outside the well-tended garden of American literature into a world of dunes. The Thoreau-inspired idealism of my youth had been transformed into a passion to understand a part of the world where I would never fit in, and to explain it to an America where I no longer fit very well either. Get it right. Be fair. You can be better than this, I told myself over and over again. One starts out where her mind takes her and then finds that a mind can't work contentedly without the heart pumping the blood of one's humanity through that mind. This, I guessed, had also been the case with Amal and the sad dilemma of child labor.

It had started, she told me, when she had seen a British television special about a British department store that sold goods made by child labor in North Africa. There was a great uproar, and the factories that sold to Britain fired all their child workers and hired adults instead. But the next summer when she visited that country, Amal had decided to trace what had happened to those children after they were fired. They were all young girls, most in their very early teens. They should have ended up back in school, but they did not, because their families didn't have money for school uniforms and books without the income the children were making from the factory. So the little girls just went back to work, this time as live-in housemaids for middle-class families. This was far worse than factory work, Amal explained, because when they were working in the factory, the children could at least live at home with their parents and work regular hours. As housemaids, they were virtual slaves, with no set times off and no family love to support them. I remembered reading Harriet Wilson's *Our Nig*, the story of a black child servant in nineteenth-century America, technically free because she did not live in a slave state, but unable to leave despite physical and emotional abuse because, as a child, she had nowhere to go. I had thought that world was long past, but it seemed it was only long past among the world's lucky. "And a couple of the little girls ended up as child prostitutes," Amal added.

I had often wondered about child labor, I told her, when I went down to the rug souks in Sharjah and Dhaid and looked at the beautiful handmade carpets to be bought rather cheaply, if one haggled. Should I really be buying those rugs? I wondered. Weren't those rugs sometimes made by children in India and Iran and Pakistan and Afghanistan because adult hands were too big to tie the tiny knots that made those rugs so beautiful and durable? I knew that, for some of the tribal people, rug making was a traditional cottage industry that supported whole families in lean times—but how could one tell the difference between the rugs made by adult craftsmen (and women) and those made by children in city factories? I told Amal about teaching Ursula Le Guin's story, "The Ones Who Walk Away from Omelas," in which one child is kept in darkness and misery so that the rest of the society can lead a charmed and prosperous life. One of my students had compared the life of the child kept in darkness to the lives of the child rug makers. "All so we can have beautiful rugs in our houses," the girl had written.

"Yes," Amal said. "But boycotting the rugs won't change that. Governments can change it, if they regulate the number of hours children can work and insist that they go to school as well, but individual people can't. I think it's hard for Americans to realize that there are terrible things that they can't change by their own efforts."

I thought of Afghanistan, where my favorite rugs came from, which at the last millennium had been a center of civilization. Now men, women, and children crippled by land mines, unable to return to farming even if all wars ended, were sitting on dirt floors tying knots for rugs. I tried to imagine a world in which American children were missing feet and starving, but I couldn't. It was indeed another world. The hunger of our delayed dinner and the cold of a chilly evening spent outdoors seemed trivial. I had known, I suppose, that safe and well-fed people like us were an anomaly in the world's population, and that sadder still, children like those happy and excited youngsters playing tag down in the camp were rare in this world too. We were moving into the twenty-first century while much of the world still struggled with the nineteenth—except that war was now more devastating.

"People are starting to form a line down there by the

kitchen," I observed. "Let's get down there before other people get there first."

When we returned to the camp, I noticed that Amal was covered with sand, and I assumed I looked the same. I had expected that the children in our group would be frantic with hunger and was surprised that they seemed only somewhat interested in the prospect of food. In fact, they were equally interested in the foodless plates that had been distributed to us and the possible uses of these plates as shields, hats, and tambourines. This mystery was solved when Anita explained that she and Mona, suspecting that food might not be served until late, had brought granola bars and chips with them.

"If you don't learn contingency planning, you don't survive motherhood," Anita explained.

I also learned some other mildly good news. Although there would not be a belly dancer performing on stage, there would be dancing for the guests. As the evening progressed, however, I found that we had music and dancing in theory more than in practice. The electrical generator wasn't powerful enough to supply us with light and sound simultaneously for more than five or ten minutes at a time. The dance floor would suddenly go pitch black, and we would hear a crash and a bellow as someone tripped over a darting eight-year old. At other times, the music cut out entirely and the lights would come on very brightly, so that one would suddenly find herself standing very close to a yet gyrating stranger coated in a rough shell of sweat and sand. Or perhaps they really weren't strangers but were merely unrecognizable in their sandman costumes, like mummers in the New Year's parade.

Later, when the music shifted from disco to Arabic pop, Anita and Mona glided in circles around each other, shoulders and hips moving to different beats in a way I've never been able to master. Arabic dancing isn't just hip movements—the dance is in the feet and the arms and the eyes as well. After a moment, I gave up trying to follow them and just watched. And so did the children, big-eyed with amazement. Anita and Mona had put their children to bed as soon as the dancing began, promising to wake them up at midnight. This night, I realized, was a night these children would be telling their grandchildren about, and they would remember how their mothers had danced.

"I remember the night the twentieth century ended," they would say, sitting comfortably in some living room of the future. "My Mama took me to a party out in the desert, and I got really sleepy, but they woke me up just as the millennium changed. I remember there was music, and I could hear it on and off, and I could look up and see the stars sometimes, which were ten times closer and brighter than they are now. And my Mama danced. She danced like a houri of paradise, and no one has danced like that ever since."

Shortly after midnight, everybody from our group was ready to go to bed. The lights and the music both went off at once, which, by this time, was a blessing. But bed, I was alarmed to learned, was the same sandbags on which we had sat with such complaint when we first arrived. The other guests continued drinking and singing, and there were loud goodbyes and louder roarings of land rovers as most of the guests from the hotel groups departed to spend the first night of the next millennium on real beds.

I tossed around for hours trying to get comfortable.

"Is that you doing all that groaning and thrashing?" came Amal's clear and utterly wide-awake voice from the sandbags next to me.

"No," I said. "It is some drunken European businessman who plans to ravish you. Of course it's me."

"If you switch the cushions around so that they are sideways rather than lengthwise, you'll be more comfortable."

I climbed out of my sleeping bag and followed her instructions, but I asked, "And how is changing the orientation of these cushions going to make them any softer?"

"It will not," she said, "but it will give you a wider space in which to thrash around and make noise and be miserable. After this, whatever happens to us in the twenty-first century is sure to be an improvement."

But as the night wore on and my fitful dreams were haunted by images of all that we had talked about, I wasn't so sure. Sometimes I saw images of children working in factories, and sometimes I dreamed of Frank Herbert's Fremen marching over endless dunes, but in my dream, somehow all of earth itself had turned into a dune planet. And yet when I was wide awake, which was much of the time, I knew that for me the next day would be better. I would go home and sleep in a bed and wash the sand out of my hair and look out my living room window at the safely stabilized dune that lay between the university gate and the Sharjah airport, a dune that I realized now was not a dune at all, but just a hill of sand. And the Emiratis and other Arabs who had come here to the desert tonight for the fun of it would go home to their jobs and to their safe clean houses, just as I would, and the tourists would go back to their own comfortable lives. Tomorrow, I would not be lying awake wondering where the hopes of my youth had gone. Twenty-five years ago, I had been sure that the twenty-first century would be a fairer and less violent time, and that my generation's efforts would bring about these changes. Now I couldn't say whether this was true. I didn't even know if this was an accurate assessment or just the cynicism of middle age, no, more than middle age, since I was unlikely to live past one hundred. This dune planet was my planet, the only one I had. The present moment was my only time, although the past and future drifted around it like sand. The people with whom I lived now were as much akin to me as the people I had lived with for the first half of my life, and the road that had begun in the hills of western Pennsylvania had carried me here, now.

I got up and walked out of the tent to look at the stars one more time, but they were obscured by the early morning fog. The bonfires had burned down to embers, and the dunes were looming gray shadows in the predawn light. Mona and Anita and their families were curled up in one corner of the tent, but one of the tousled heads suddenly moved, and a sleepy-eyed little girl was looking at me, curious. The winding sandy track would lead her out from this time and place into a new millennium and a whole new set of memories and people and places. For that one instant, I was part of that inner space that stretched across a lifespan.